W9-BTR-426

Mary
and the Saints

Mary and the Saints

Companions on the Journey

Catholic Basics
A Pastoral Ministry Series

James P. Campbell, D. Min.

Thomas P. Walters, Ph.D.
Series Editor

NATIONAL CONFERENCE FOR
CATECHETICAL LEADERSHIP

LOYOLA PRESS.
A JESUIT MINISTRY
Chicago

LOYOLA PRESS.
A JESUIT MINISTRY

3441 N. Ashland Avenue
Chicago, Illinois 60657
(800) 621-1008
www.loyolapress.com

NIHIL OBSTAT: Rev. Daniel J. Mahan, S.T.B., S.T.L.
Censor Librorum

IMPRIMATUR: Rev. Msgr. Joseph F. Schaedel
Vicar General/Moderator of the Curia

Given at Indianapolis, Indiana, on February 19, 2001

The *nihil obstat* and *imprimatur* are official declarations that a book is free of doctrinal and moral error. No implication is contained herein that those who have granted the *nihil obstat* and *imprimatur* agree with the content, opinions, or statements expressed.

Acknowledgments appearing on page 92 constitute a continuation of the copyright page

Cover Design: Other Brother Design
Cover Illustration: Steve Snodgrass
Interior Illustrations: Other Brother Design

Library of Congress Cataloging-in-Publication Data
Campbell, James P.
Mary and the saints : companions on the journey / James P. Campbell.
p. cm. – (Catholic basics)
Rev. ed. of: Companion on the journey.
Includes bibliographical references.
ISBN-13: 978-0-8294-1725-8
ISBN-10: 0-8294-1725-7
1. Mary, Blessed Virgin, Saint. 2. Christian saints. 3. Pastoral theology–
Catholic Church. I. Campbell, James P. Companions on the journey. II. Title.
III. Series.
BT605.2 .C36 2001
235'.2–dc21   2001029699
                                                               CIP

Published by Loyola Press, 3441 N. Ashland Avenue, Chicago, Illinois 60657 U.S.A.
© 2002 The National Conference for Catechetical Leadership.

All rights reserved. No part of this book may be reproduced, stored in a retrieval system, or transmitted in any form or by any means, electronic, mechanical, photocopying, recording, or otherwise, without the prior permission of the publisher.

Manufactured in the United States of America.
08 09 10 11 12 Bang 10 9 8 7 6 5 4

Table of Contents

About the Series

Catholic Basics: A Pastoral Ministry Series offers an in-depth yet accessible understanding of the fundamentals of the Catholic faith for adults, both those preparing for lay ministry and those interested in the topics for their own personal growth. The series helps readers explore the Catholic tradition and apply what they have learned to their lives and ministry situations. Each title offers a reliable introduction to a specific topic and provides a foundational understanding of the concepts.

Each book in the series presents a Catholic understanding of its topic as found in Scripture and the teachings of the Church. Each of the authors has paid special attention to the documents of the Second Vatican Council and the *Catechism of the Catholic Church*, so that further learning can be guided by these core resources.

Chapters conclude with study questions that may be used for small group review or for individual reflection. Additionally, suggestions for further reading offer dependable guides for extra study.

The initiative of the National Conference of Catechetical Leadership led to the development of an earlier version of this series. The indispensable contribution of the series editor, Dr. Thomas Walters, helped ensure that the concepts and ideas presented here are easily accessible to a wide audience.

Certification Standards: National Resources for Church Ministry

E ach book in this theology series relates to standards for theological competency identified in the resources listed below. Three national church ministry organizations provide standards for certification programs that serve their respective ministries. The standards were developed in collaboration with the United States Catholic Conference Commission on Certification and Accreditation. The fourth resource is the latest document, and it was developed to identify common goals of the three sets of standards.

Competency Based Certification Standards for Pastoral Ministers, Pastoral Associates and Parish Life Coordinators. Chicago: National Association for Lay Ministry, Inc. (NALM), 1994.

These standards address three roles found in pastoral ministry settings in the United States. The standards were the earliest to receive approval from the United States Catholic Conference Commission on Certification and Accreditation. Copies of the standards are available from the National Association for Lay Ministry, 5420 S. Cornell, Chicago, IL 60615-5604.

National Certification Standards for Professional Parish Directors of Religious Education. Washington, DC: National Conference for Catechetical Leadership, 1998.

NCCL developed standards to foster appropriate initial education and formation, as well as continuing personal and professional development, of those who serve as Directors of Religious Education (DREs). The standards address various areas of knowledge and abilities needed in the personal, theological, and professional aspects of the ministry. Also included is a code of ethics for professional catechetical leaders. Available from the National Conference of Catechetical Leadership, 3021 Fourth Street NE, Washington, DC 20017-1102.

NFCYM Competency-Based Standards for the Coordinator of Youth Ministry. Washington, DC: National Federation for Catholic Youth Ministry, 1996.

This document lays out the wide range of knowledge and skills that support ministry with young people as well as the successful leadership and organization of youth ministry wherever it may be situated. The standards are available from the National Federation for Catholic Youth Ministry, 415 Michigan Avenue NE, Suite 40, Washington, DC 20017-1518.

Merkt, Joseph T., ed. *Common Formation Goals for Ministry.* A joint publication of NALM, NFCYM, and NCCL, 2000.

Rev. Joseph Merkt compared the documentation of standards cited by three national organizations serving pastoral, youth, and catechetical ministries. The resulting statement of common goals identifies common ground for those who prepare persons for ministry, as well as for the many people who wear multiple hats. Copies are available from NALM, NCCL, or NFCYM.

Introduction

M any of the most touching images in the Catholic imagination are those of the Blessed Virgin Mary and of favorite saints. We imagine, for example, the young Mary facing an angel who asks her to make a choice not only for herself but for the world as well or the image of a sorrowful mother at the foot of the cross. We also imagine the saints and their heroic love for God and others: the joy of St. Francis of Assisi preaching to the birds; the sacrifice of St. Maximillian Kolbe giving up his life so another can live; and the steadfast faith of St. Thérèse of Lisieux, whose "little way" gives modern Christians an accessible means to travel the path to holiness.

Pope John Paul II wrote a post-synodal apostolic exhortation on the Church in America, *Ecclesia in America (EA)*. In chapter 1, "The Encounter with the Living Jesus Christ," the Holy Father writes about the important role of devotions to Mary and the saints in American spiritual life (11). The life of devotion is intense and takes place in all levels of society. The devotions are carried out in practices such as pilgrimages to shrines of Mary and the saints; the use of sacramentals like water, oil, and candles; and the popular devotion of praying the Rosary. The pope notes that these forms of piety are important ways in which the faithful can learn both genuine spiritual values leading to a life of conversion and practical ways to care for others. When practiced within the context of the life of the Church, they lead to the inculturation of Christian values in the local cultures.

The *General Directory for Catechesis (GDC)* also acknowledges that the devotional life is a "vital dimension in Catholic life." Popular devotions to the saints can arouse in the faithful a capacity for self-dedication and even heroism in professing the faith. Through popular devotions, people can arrive at a "keen sensitivity" to the virtues of God: "his fatherly compassion, his providence, his benevolence and loving presence" (#195, as quoted from *Evangelii Nuntiandi [EN], On Evangelization in the Modern World*, #48). When devotions are prayed in balance,

> [they] can develop in the inmost depths of man habits of virtue rarely to be found otherwise in the same degree, such as patience, acceptance of the Cross in daily life, detachment, openness to other men and a spirit of ready service.
>
> (*GDC*, #195, as quoted from *EN*, #48)

When not prayed in the context of the teaching of the Church, however, devotions can lead to "dangers arising out of its errors or fanaticism, superstition, syncretism, or religious ignorance . . ."(#195, as quoted from *EN*, #48). This caution extends to devotions to Mary: Certain forms of Marian devotion . . . , because of long usage, require a renewed catechesis to restore to them elements that have become lost or obscured (*GDC*, #196).

This book gives a short outline of the origins of the devotions to Mary and the saints, the way in which saints are proclaimed today, and the place apparitions of Mary have in the context of the Church. The hope is that readers will find here a resource that will help explain the place of Mary and the saints within the context of the life of the Church.

CHAPTER 1

Mary in the New Testament

When we consider the great impact Mary has had on the history of Christian spirituality, and the impact she continues to have on the daily life of Christians today, we can be surprised that there is so little written about her in the New Testament. In fact, there are more verses about Mary in the Qu?an, the sacred text of Islam, than there are in the New Testament, where Mary appears in the four Gospels and the Acts of the Apostles.

Mary in the Gospel of Mark

In the Gospel of Mark, there are no scenes in which Mary appears alone. She appears only once in company with the rest of her family (Mark 3:21, 31–35) at a point in Jesus' life when he is beginning his ministry to a wider audience. His family appears embarrassed with his activities and attempts to take him home: "When his family heard it, they went out to restrain him, for people were saying, 'He has gone out of his mind'" (Mark 3:21).

Later in the chapter, while Jesus is preaching, his family once again gathers and calls for him. When the crowd tells him of his family's presence, he replies:

> "Who are my mother and my brothers?" And look-
> ing at those who sat around him, he said, "Here are
> my mother and my brothers! Whoever does the will
> of God is my brother and sister and mother."
>
> (Mark 3:33–35)

This scene, in which Jesus presents the importance and intimacy of discipleship, does not instill in readers a desire to form a close relationship with Mary. Neither is Mark's critical outlook alleviated at 6:1–6, when the locals at Nazareth are astounded at Jesus' religious prominence: "'Is not this the carpenter, the son of Mary and brother of James and Joses and Judas and Simon, and are not his sisters here with us?'" (Mark 6:3).

In response, Jesus says that a prophet is not at home in his own country, and leaves his hometown for the wider world. Again, these events do little to convey a positive image of Mary.

Mary in the Gospel of Matthew

In Matthew's Gospel, Mark's dismissal of Mary along with the other blood relatives of Jesus is softened with a greater recognition of her position in the mystery of salvation. Matthew does not present Mary in a direct way. Rather, Matthew presents her through the story of Joseph's calling by an angel to his vocation as Jesus' guardian.

> Now the birth of Jesus the Messiah took place in this way. When his mother Mary had been engaged to Joseph, but before they lived together, she was found to be with child from the Holy Spirit. Her husband Joseph, being a righteous man and unwilling to expose her to public disgrace, planned to dismiss her quietly. But just when he had resolved to do this, an angel of the Lord appeared to him in a dream and said, "Joseph, son of David, do not be afraid to take Mary as your wife, for the child conceived in her is from the Holy Spirit. She will bear a son, and you are to name him Jesus, for he will save his people from their sins." All this took place to fulfill what had been spoken by the Lord through the prophet:
>
> "Look, the virgin shall conceive and bear a son,
>   and they shall name him Emmanuel,"
> which means, "God is with us."
> When Joseph awoke from sleep, he did as the angel of the Lord commanded him; he took her as his wife, but had no marital relations with her

*until she had borne a son; and he named him
Jesus.*

(Matthew 1:18–25)

The angel reveals to Joseph that Jesus is Emmanuel, "God with us," the fulfillment of the greatest hopes of Israel. The role of Mary is also revealed as that of a virgin who is totally dedicated to God, living in intimate relationship with the Holy Spirit.

In proclaiming that Jesus was born of Mary, Matthew emphasizes Jesus' humanity and places him within the context of the Jewish faith. He also emphasizes Mary's role as a partner with God in fulfilling his plan for the salvation of humankind from all eternity. Mary was the pinnacle of the faith of Israel in its relationship with God.

Matthew softens the image of Mary as found in Mark. Mary is not just the blood mother of Jesus who is left behind as Jesus fulfills the requirements of his ministry. She is the Virgin Mother of Israel, the one who is related to the Holy Spirit, the one who, through her cooperation with God, provides the possibility of Israel's hope.

Mary in the Gospel of Luke

The Gospel of Luke is the primary source for the warm images of Mary that are most popular in the Catholic world. While Mary receives passing mention in the Gospels of Mark and Matthew, she is a principal player in Luke.

THE ANNUNCIATION

In Luke, Mary first appears at 1:26–38. She is a teenage girl greeted by an angel who tells her that she will be the mother of the Messiah. In Jewish culture of this time, the normal age for betrothal was soon after a girl's twelfth birthday.

Mary is no doubt puzzled by the angel's greeting: "Greetings, favored one! The Lord is with you" (Luke 1:28).

The greeting, translated by St. Jerome in the Latin Vulgate as "full of grace," implies the giving of unmerited favor from one who is all-powerful to someone who receives it as blessing. It is a sign of God's willingness to form a special, personal relationship with Mary, who is his choice and love.

The angel then informs Mary of the nature of the special relationship God is entering into with her.

> The angel said to her, "Do not be afraid, Mary, for you have found favor with God. And now, you will conceive in your womb and bear a son, and you will name him Jesus. He will be great, and will be called the Son of the Most High, and the Lord God will give to him the throne of his ancestor David. He will reign over the house of Jacob forever, and of his kingdom there will be no end."
>
> (Luke 1:30–33)

When Mary asks how this will be done since she is a virgin, the angel replies:

> "The Holy Spirit will come upon you, and the power of the Most High will overshadow you; therefore the child to be born will be holy; he will be called Son of God." (1:35)

Mary is the first to hear that the promise of salvation—the promise that is the hope for her people and for the world—will be fulfilled. She responds, "'Here am I, the servant of the Lord; let it be with me according to your word.' Then the angel departed from her" (Luke 1:38).

Mary gives God her absolute consent—and in giving her consent, she becomes the first and most faithful of Jesus' disciples.

THE VISITATION

Mary, having learned from the angel of Elizabeth's pregnancy, goes to visit her in Judah, a week's walk from Nazareth. Mary's kindness and concern for Elizabeth are seen in her immediate decision to visit her cousin and share the good news with her. As Mary arrives, Elizabeth is moved by the Spirit to proclaim her blessed among women:

> And Elizabeth was filled with the Holy Spirit and exclaimed with a loud cry, "Blessed are you among women, and blessed is the fruit of your womb. And why has this happened to me, that the mother of my Lord comes to me? For as soon as I heard the sound of your greeting, the child in my womb leaped for joy. And blessed is she who believed that there would be a fulfillment of what was spoken to her by the Lord." (1:41–45)

Elizabeth's acclamation is important for a number of reasons. For the first time in Luke's Gospel, the title "Lord" is used for Jesus. It is the word used in Greek to translate the name of God, Yahweh. It is a name for God that is full of awe and mystery.

Elizabeth recognizes Mary's blessedness on two accounts. First, because Mary has accepted God's will that she be the mother of the Messiah; second, because Mary has believed. She has become the model of what it means to be a disciple.

THE MAGNIFICAT

Mary's response to Elizabeth has been for centuries the source of inspiration for artists, musicians, and poets. It is also her song that is sung every day in the prayer of the Church.

> And Mary said,
> "My soul magnifies the Lord,
>   and my spirit rejoices in God my Savior,
> for he has looked with favor on the lowliness of his servant.
>   Surely, from now on all generations will call me blessed;
> for the Mighty One has done great things for me,
>   and holy is his name.

His mercy is for those who fear him
from generation to generation.
He has shown strength with his arm;
he has scattered the proud in the thoughts of their
hearts.
He has brought down the powerful from their thrones,
and lifted up the lowly;
he has filled the hungry with good things,
and sent the rich away empty.
He has helped his servant Israel,
in remembrance of his mercy,
according to the promise he made to our ancestors,
to Abraham and to his descendants forever."

And Mary remained with her about three months and
then returned to her home. (1:46–56)

Mary's response to Elizabeth's proclamation reflects the meaning of her life and the memory of the early Church regarding what she means to the Christian community. Mary's song is one of rejoicing in the action of God—in the history of Israel and in her life. The song reflects the Exodus experience, when the Hebrews were a hated and despised people who were freed from slavery. It reflects their experience in the desert, where they were totally dependent on God. In the period of the judges the spirit came on charismatic individuals who fought for the people. In times of wealth the ruling classes of Israel and Judah themselves became the oppressors of the poor. But the experience of the Babylonian captivity again reminded the people that they were totally dependent on God. The later books of the Old Testament show dependence on God for love and mercy as the central theme of Jewish spirituality.

Mary's prayer summarizes the needs of the poor. It shows what it means to be confident in the power of God's mercy from generation to generation. The proud are scattered, and the mighty are brought down from their thrones. The hungry are fed, and the rich are sent away empty. More than any other single passage, the Magnificat shows Mary as a symbol of hope and a sign of God's care for the needy and helpless in this world.

THE BIRTH OF JESUS

Mary remains a major figure in Luke's Gospel through the narratives of Jesus' birth and early years. The shepherds and other witnesses are amazed at the events surrounding Jesus' birth—and Mary treasures the events in her heart (see Luke 2:19). When Mary and Joseph take Jesus to be presented in the Temple, Mary hears from Simeon that her own life will not be without pain:

> Then Simeon blessed them and said to [Jesus'] mother Mary, "This child is destined for the falling and the rising of many in Israel, and to be a sign that will be opposed so that the inner thoughts of many will be revealed—and a sword will pierce your own soul too." (2:34–35)

Mary's sorrow is evident in the final scene of the Luke infancy narrative, when Jesus reaches the age of twelve. Mary and Joseph have come with Jesus to Jerusalem on pilgrimage. When they are returning home, Mary and Joseph discover that Jesus is missing. They return to Jerusalem and, after three days, discover Jesus speaking with the elders in the Temple.

> When his parents saw him they were astonished; and his mother said to him, "Child, why have you treated us like this? Look, your father and I have been searching for you in great anxiety." He said to them, "Why were you searching for me? Did you not know that I must be in my Father's house?" But they did not understand what he said to them. Then he went down with them and came to Nazareth, and was obedient to them. His mother treasured all these things in her heart. (2:48–51)

THE FAITHFUL DISCIPLE

The incident between Jesus and his family that we saw in Mark 3:21, 31–35 loses its bite in Luke's Gospel. When Jesus' family comes to where he is teaching, and he learns that they are there, he says to the crowd, "My mother and my brothers are those who hear the word of God and do it" (Luke 8:21). In Luke, Jesus' mother and relatives are considered faithful disciples, showing up at Pentecost among the believers awaiting the coming of the Holy Spirit (see Acts 1:13–14).

Mary in the Gospel of John

The Gospel of John contains two important passages in which Mary appears. She first appears in the marriage at Cana, where she is instrumental in the beginnings of Jesus' ministry. She then appears at the foot of the cross, where she is named the Mother of the Church.

THE MARRIAGE AT CANA

In John's Gospel, the wedding feast at Cana is the beginning of Jesus' public ministry. Jesus and his disciples have been invited to the wedding of a family friend. In the course of the celebration, Mary discovers that the family will be short of wine, which will be a major embarrassment to them.

> Jesus and his disciples had also been invited to the wedding. When the wine gave out, the mother of Jesus said to him, "They have no wine." And Jesus said to her, "Woman, what concern is that to you and to me? My hour has not yet come." His mother said to the servants, "Do whatever he tells you." Now standing there were six stone water jars for the Jewish rites of purification, each holding twenty or thirty gallons. Jesus said to them, "Fill the jars with water." And they filled them up to the brim. He said to them, "Now draw some out, and take it to the chief steward." So they took it. When the steward tasted the water that had become wine, and did not know where it came from (though the servants who had

drawn the water knew), the steward called the bride-groom and said to him, "Everyone serves the good wine first, and then the inferior wine after the guests have become drunk. But you have kept the good wine until now." Jesus did this, the first of his signs, in Cana of Galilee, and revealed his glory; and his disciples believed in him. (2:2–11)

The wedding scene of Cana is John's story of Jesus' introduction to his ministry. In this introduction, the "mother of Jesus" plays a decisive role. She serves as the one who helps Jesus make the transition into his public ministry. Jesus' objection that his hour has not yet come is met with Mary's silent faith, and she initiates the event that will lead to his final hour. Mary is present at the beginning of Jesus' ministry, as she will be at the end, when Jesus is glorified through his death on the cross.

Jesus addresses Mary as "woman." She is addressed as "woman" again at the crucifixion (John 19:25–27). This could mean that John is alluding to Mary as the new Eve, who was called "mother of all the living" (Genesis 3:20). Mary will be seen as the mother of all who live in faith.

THE CRUCIFIXION

As we have seen, John also presents Mary at the scene of Jesus' final hour, his death on the cross.

Meanwhile, standing near the cross of Jesus were his mother, and his mother's sister, Mary the wife of Clopas, and Mary Magdalene. When Jesus saw his mother and the disciple whom he loved standing beside her, he said to his mother, "Woman, here is your son." Then he said to the disciple, "Here is your mother." And from that hour the disciple took her into his own home. (19:25–27)

We have seen the relationship of Mary to Eve, a theme that we will see again, as the mother of the living in the New Covenant. Jesus reveals Mary as the mother of the disciples. It is clear that there is a spiritual dimension to Mary's role in the economy of salvation. All of Jesus' disciples will also be "sons of Mary."

Brothers and Sisters of Jesus?

From ancient times, the Church has believed that Jesus was Mary's only child and that Mary was perpetually a virgin. Yet the Gospels talk about Jesus' "brother's and sisters." The *Catechism of the Catholic Church (CCC)* comments:

> Against this doctrine the objection is sometimes raised that the Bible mentions brothers and sisters of Jesus (cf. Mark 3:31–35; 6:3; 1 Corinthians 9:5; Galatians 1:19). The Church has always understood these passages as not referring to other children of the Virgin Mary. In fact James and Joseph, "brothers of Jesus," are the sons of another Mary, a disciple of Christ, whom St. Matthew significantly calls "the other Mary" (Matthew 13:55; 28:1, cf. Matthew 27:56).They are close relations of Jesus, according to an Old Testament expression (cf. Genesis 13:8; 14:16; 29:15; etc.). (#500)

SVMMARY

In the New Testament, we see that Mary is presented in a variety of ways. In the Gospel of Mark, there is no individual portrait of Mary, and she is presented with Jesus' relatives who seem to be embarrassed with his ministry. Matthew presents Mary as a partner with Joseph, cooperating with God to bring about the salvation of the human race.

In the Gospel of Luke, Mary is presented in her full glory as the one on whose decision the future of the salvation of humankind depends (Luke 1:26–38). Luke also presents Mary as speaking for the needs of the poor and outcast (Luke 1:46–56). She is the witness of faith who ponders in her heart all of the events surrounding Jesus' birth (Luke 2:48–51). This is the image of Mary that warms the heart of Christians who see in her the model of Christian discipleship.

In the Gospel of John, Mary is presented as the new Eve, who helps initiate Jesus' ministry at the wedding at Cana (John 2:2–11), and who is present at the foot of the cross (John 19:25–27), where Jesus proclaims that she will be the mother of all his disciples.

The number of verses on Mary in the Bible is relatively few. But the images that they describe are the foundation of the Church's theological reflection on Mary and will continue to be the source for artists and writers who reflect on the meaning of Mary's life for all generations.

FOR REFLECTION

1. Mary made a decision in faith as a young woman. When the direction of your own life was unclear, how did you hear God calling you?

2. Mary's song, the Magnificat, describes God's concern for the poor, the outcast, and others on the margins of society and is a warning to those who would use power to make others suffer. How can you identify with the poor who are God's chief concern? How might you use your own power over others in ways that are not pleasing to God? (Consider, for example, those for whom you may have responsibility, such as a spouse, children, aging parents, students, or coworkers.)

3. Mary acted in faith at the wedding at Cana. In what ways have you experienced God responding unexpectedly and generously?

CHAPTER 2

The Deepening Understanding of Mary in the Early Church

Apocryphal stories are those writings on biblical subjects that appeared between 100 B.C. and 400 A.D. These writings, such as *The Gospel of the Ebionites, The Gospel of Philip,* and *The Infancy Gospel of Thomas,* covered much of the same material found in the Bible. They also supported heretical teachings about Jesus and were, therefore, excluded from the canon of Scripture. However, they provided images of great importance in the development of Christian art and legend.

One of the more important of the apocryphal writings is *The Book of James,* originally titled *The Nativity of Mary.* In *The Book of James,* we find the names of Mary's parents, Joachim and Anne. We also find that Mary was a child of their old age whom they dedicated to God. Joseph is presented as an aged widower with children, a man who is chosen for Mary in a miraculous way. Two feasts of Mary find their origins in *The Book of James*: the feasts of Immaculate Conception and the Birth of Mary.

The Development of the Doctrine of Mary

As the Church entered into the Greek world, Christians moved theologically from the concrete world of Jewish life to the speculative world of Greek thought. The greatest challenge to the Gospel was the Greek tendency to see the spiritual world as the ideal and the physical world as corrupt. The desire of the human spirit, according to the Greeks, was to leave this material world behind and to raise the soul to the realm of the spirit from which it came.

Thus some Greek Christians began to interpret the Gospels in a way that accentuated the spiritual at the expense of the material. This had special ramifications in terms of the identity of Jesus Christ and the role of Mary in human salvation.

Many Greek Christians could not believe that God had come in human flesh. The idea of the unity between the divine and the human in Jesus Christ offended them. So instead of teaching that Jesus was truly human, they taught that Jesus only "seemed" to be human. As a result, the Greek verb "to seem" (*dokare*) became the root word of the heresy called Docetism, which taught that Jesus only "seemed" to be human, only "seemed" to eat and drink, only "seemed" to die on the cross. To use a modern analogy, they would say that Jesus was a hologram, a three-dimensional image created by light, having no substance.

Teachers in the early Church defended the Gospel by reasserting the humanity of Jesus and insisting on the role of the Virgin Mary in the plan of salvation.

Early Church Fathers on Mary

SAINT JUSTIN MARTYR

We find an example of the Church's defense against Docetism in the work of the early Christian apologist St. Justin Martyr (+165). Justin defined the full humanity of Jesus, appealing to the Virgin Birth as a proof that Jesus Christ was the "first-born Word of God . . . at the same time man" (Grassi, *Mary: Mother & Disciple*, p. 109). Justin also taught the importance of Mary in recreating humanity's relationship with God after the sin of Eve:

> For Eve, being a virgin and undefiled, having conceived the word from the serpent, brought forth disobedience and death. The Virgin Mary, however, having received faith and joy, when the angel Gabriel announced to her the good tidings . . . answered: Be it done to me according to thy word."
> (Cunneen, *In Search of Mary*, p. 64)

In this passage, Justin reflects on Mary's role in the economy of salvation as the one who, through her obedience, made possible the victory over the serpent.

SAINT IRENAEUS OF LYON

Irenaeus, Bishop of Lyons (+202) was another important witness to the Christian faith in the early Church. Irenaeus was an important defender of the faith, especially against the Gnostics, who believed that there was a spiritual spark in the human soul seeking to return to heaven, leaving the body to disintegrate. The Gnostics taught that only a few divine souls could make the journey back to heaven, where they would receive the secret knowledge that they were among the few souls to be saved.

Following the lead of the Docetists, the Gnostics denied that Jesus Christ was God united with the human. They also taught that Jesus was a phantasm who did not suffer and die as the Gospels proclaim.

To refute the teaching that Jesus was not fully human, Irenaeus repeatedly wrote of the role of Mary and the Virgin Birth of Jesus, continuing and developing the theology of Mary as the new Eve:

> Just as Eve, wife of Adam yes, yet still a virgin . . .
> became by her disobedience the cause of death for
> herself and the whole human race, so Mary too,
> espoused yet a virgin, became by her obedience
> the cause of salvation for herself and the whole
> human race. . . . And so it was that the knot of Eve's
> disobedience was loosed by Mary's obedience.
> (Coyle, *Mary in the Christian Tradition*, p. 83)

SAINT AMBROSE OF MILAN

As the Church became accepted in the Roman Empire, the understanding of Mary developed in the works of the bishops and theologians of the Western Empire. Another view of Mary is provided in the work of St. Ambrose of Milan (339–397). For Ambrose, Mary revealed the first fruits of redemption:

> Nor is it to be wondered at that when the Lord was
> about to redeem the world, he began this work from
> Mary, so that she, through whom salvation was

being prepared for all, should be the first to draw salvation from her son.

(O'Carroll, Theotokos, p. 19)

Ambrose was also the first figure in the Western Church to call Mary "the Mother of God":

> So pure was the Blessed Mary that she was chosen to be the Mother of the Lord; God made her whom He had chosen and chose her for whom He would be made.
>
> (Supple, Virgin Wholly Marvelous, p. 46)

SAINT AUGUSTINE OF HIPPO

Another important figure in the Western Church's teaching about Mary was St. Augustine, bishop of Hippo (354–430). Augustine developed the idea of the closeness of Mary to Christ and Christ's likeness to her:

> Mary was chosen as Mother, predestined before all creatures, filled with all grace, all virtue, all holiness, to the end that of a Mother most pure might be born the Son infinitely pure. And as in Heaven the Son has a Father immortal and eternal, so on earth the Son, according to the flesh, is like the Mother. In Heaven He is eternal and immense with the Father; on earth, like the Mother, He is in time and full of meekness. In Heaven He is the image of the Father; on earth He is the likeness of His Mother.
>
> (Virgin Wholly Marvelous, p. 56)

Mary as *Theotokos*

While Mary was being praised as the Mother of God in the West, the Greek-speaking world of the East had problems using the title (see *Theotokos*). The catalyst for the issue was the teaching of

Nestorius (+451), patriarch of Constantinople, the second most important diocese in the Church. Nestorius was concerned that some thinkers had exalted the divinity of Christ to the extent that Christ's humanity was lost in the process. Instead, Nestorius wished to highlight that the complete divine person, or Logos, came to dwell in human flesh, and was therefore fully human. Mary then could not be called *Theotokos*, Mother of God, but rather should be called *Christokos*, or Mother of Christ.

Nestorius provoked more controversy while presiding over the liturgical celebration of the feast of Mary in his cathedral. The preacher, Proclus, gave a stirring sermon on the qualities of Mary, finally proclaiming that Mary was the *Theotokos*. At this point, Nestorius left his cathedral seat and went to the pulpit. Contradicting Proclus, Nestorius said that while Mary was entitled to all praises, she could not be called *Theotokos*. Mary, Nestorius reasoned, was not the Mother of the Eternal Word. Only the human Christ was born in her womb. Nestorius believed that Christ was a human person who was joined to the divine person of God's Son. Therefore, there were two persons in Christ: the divine person and the human person. Mary could only be called the mother of the human person.

Nestorius's intervention caused a scandal, and the news of his words and actions spread throughout the Mediterranean Church. The pope condemned Nestorius in a letter that he sent through Cyril of Alexandria (375–444), an enemy of Nestorius. The issue for the pope and for Cyril was the separation of the divine and the human in Jesus Christ, causing a separation that denied the Incarnation. Cyril insisted that while there were two natures in Christ, there was only one Person, a position later confirmed at the Council of Chalcedon (451).

Cyril called for an ecumenical council, which met in Ephesus in 431. Using his influence, Cyril excluded Nestorius's supporters. Nestorius was deposed as bishop and excommunicated, and Mary was proclaimed *Theotokos*. In the proclamation, the Council of Ephesus taught that Mary had truly become the Mother of God by the human conception of God in her womb.

"Mother of God, not that the nature of the Word or his divinity received the beginning of its existence from the holy Virgin, but that, since the holy body, animated by a rational soul, which the Word of God united to himself according to the hypostasis, was born from her, the Word is said to be born according to the flesh."

(Council of Ephesus, as quoted in *CCC*, #466)

The bishops in Ephesus emphasized the meaning of the Incarnation. Mary is not Mother of God in terms of Christ's divinity. But when the Word united himself to humanity by being born of Mary, the Word can be said to have been born of the flesh. Since divine nature and human nature are united in Jesus Christ, Mary can be said to be the Mother of God.

The victorious Cyril was eloquent in his praise of Mary:

Hail Mary, Mother of God, majestic common-treasure of the whole world, the lamp unquenchable, the crown of virginity, the scepter of orthodoxy, the indissoluble temple, the dwelling of the Illimitable, Mother and Virgin . . . through whom Angels and Archangels rejoice, devils are put to flight . . . and the fallen creature is received up into the heavens.

(*In Search of Mary*, p. 133)

On hearing of this victory for Mary, the people of Ephesus responded with wild rejoicing. Cyril and his followers were led to their apartments by crowds carrying torches and crying out, "Praised be the *Theotokos*! Long live Cyril!" A new church was dedicated to Mary over the ruins of the temple of Diana, the goddess of the Ephesians.

In the process, Mary was raised from the image of a humble handmaid of the Lord, to the regal status of the Mother of God. New churches were built in her honor, and new feast days were added to the liturgical calendar. In Christian art she was now clothed in the robes of an Eastern empress, wearing pearls, earrings, and the crown of royalty.

The proclamation helped to foster the idea of the Assumption of Mary into heaven, where she could be invoked for healing and protection. As the lordly figure of Christ became more distant to the people, Mary began to take over some of her son's functions as intermediary between God and humankind.

Summary

Reflection on Mary in the early Church revolved primarily around the role of Mary as Jesus' mother. As the Christian faith moved into the Greek and Roman worlds, there was the danger of losing Christ's humanity and his becoming a spiritual figure only. Early Christian thinkers emphasized that by giving birth to Jesus Mary cooperated in repairing the damage that had been inflicted on humankind by Adam and Eve.

Finally, at the Council of Ephesus (431) Mary is declared to be the Mother of God. This declaration will lead to the building of many churches in her honor and the promotion of devotion to Mary, who is now seen as queen of heaven who will intercede for the needs of her children.

For Reflection

1. Early Church teachers were passionately concerned that the people understand the implications of the Incarnation and Mary's role in human salvation. Meditating on Mary's position as God's choice to be the mother of the Savior causes you to think . . .

2. From the early times in Christian history, people have tried to negate the importance of Jesus' human nature. In reflecting on the role of Mary in human salvation, what are the implications of this denial?

3. Nestorius sought to deny that Mary was the Mother of God. This teaching about Mary as the Mother of God was affirmed at Ephesus. Contemplating Mary's title and its implications for your life leads you to think . . .

CHAPTER 3

Saints in the Early Church

The early centuries of the Church saw the development of the doctrines that have helped deepen our understanding of Mary. In these same centuries we see the emergence of the practice of the veneration of martyrs and other Christian heroes as intercessors for the people before God.

The early Christian Church entered a hostile world. As Christianity spread into the Roman world, the disciples first went to Jewish synagogues that were in most of the major cities of the empire. There they proclaimed the coming of the Messiah. This led to unrest among the Jewish communities. In Jerusalem the hostility led to the killing of James, the first Christian bishop, and to the increasing isolation of the Christians from the Jewish community. As described in the Acts of the Apostles and the letters of Paul, early Christians found their converts and established their communities among the Greek-speaking gentile communities.

Because Judaism was an accepted religion in the Roman Empire, Jews were free to assemble for worship. The political situation in Palestine between 60 and 70 was unstable, however, leading to war and invasion by Roman armies. Palestine was devastated, with Jerusalem and the Temple being destroyed in the year 70.

Jewish leaders struggled to re-establish their identity as a religious community. Scholars believe that Jewish religious leaders met in the Palestinian village of Jamnia around the year 90. In the process of creating the foundations of modern Judaism, they made a number of decisions. The Jewish leaders decided that the Messiah had not yet come and made this position a point of identification for all who would call themselves Jewish. This had the effect of excluding Christians from the synagogue. As a result, the Christian Church found itself an illegal association in the Roman Empire; Christian worship and assembly became illegal.

Martyrs in Early Christendom

Beginning with Nero's persecution of the Christian Church in Rome (ca. 65), and lasting through the Edict of Milan (313),

Christians lived under scrutiny. While the periods of systematic persecution were relatively few, Christians were outsiders and considered atheists because they did not celebrate the festivals of the local gods. If crops failed or other natural disasters happened, invariably, cities would hear the cry "Christians to the lions!" This created the conditions that led to the first Christian heroes.

The earliest Christian heroes were the "martyrs." The Greek word for martyr means "witness." Those who were ready to die for the faith were celebrated as martyrs.

There were, of course, Old Testament examples of such martyrs. During the period of Greek persecution of the Jews (175 B.C.–135 B.C.), for example, there was Eleazer, the scribe who died rather than eat the pork his persecutors tried to force on him (see 2 Maccabees 6:18–31). In the same period we also find the story of the mother and her seven sons who died, one after the other, rather than break the covenant (see 2 Maccabees 7:1–41). The accounts of Jesus' suffering and death in the Gospels and the martyrdom of Stephen (see Acts 6:8–7:60) are the important New Testament examples of martyrs.

Martyrdom was seen as a charism in the early Church; however, not all Christians were called to be martyrs. A Christian could not simply approach the authorities to confess membership in the faith in the hope of being put to death. This would be suicide and would place the authorities in the position of murderers. Commenting on the charism of martyrdom, St. Augustine said that the intention of the martyrs was to witness to their faith. They were willing to die as a consequence of believing in Jesus.

Martyrs saw the giving of their lives as a kind of second Baptism, their passion a participation in the Passion of Christ. Confessing their faith to the death, they showed the Roman state that there were values that transcended the power of the Roman Empire and its gods. Because they died for Christ, martyrs were seen as able to forgive sins in the name of Christ, both in this life and later in heaven. Unbaptized persons who died for the sake of the Christian faith were seen as baptized in the giving of their own blood.

The major periods of persecution were from 251 to 313. Relatively few Christians, however, actually suffered and died for the faith. Many fell away from the faith, and others went into hiding. Therefore, martyrs, as heroes to the Church, were held in high regard.

The Practice of Veneration of Martyrs

Beginning in the third century, the practice of veneration of the martyrs spread throughout the Church. The martyrs were celebrated in memory, and their gravesites became shrines.

Martyrdom was an imitation and participation in the suffering of Christ. Christ was present with the martyrs, strengthening them. Martyrs were also seen as fighting the devil and his helpers, and the victories of the martyrs were seen as victories of grace over the intentions of evil spirits.

Tertullian (ca. 160–ca. 225), an early Church father, described martyrdom as Baptism in blood bringing forgiveness of sins. Martyrdom was also seen as a witness to the Roman state of its subordination to the God of heaven and for unbelievers to the truth of the Gospel. Martyrs were seen as perfect disciples who immediately realized the blessings promised to all Christians. As such, they were believed to have entered into heaven immediately rather than having to pass through intermediate stages.

Martyrs as Intercessors

Living with Christ in heaven, martyrs were seen to have direct access to God. Therefore, they could act as intercessors and pray for the needs of those left behind. They were not seen as having any power in their own right, but as servants of Christ and mediators of grace.

Greeks and Romans celebrated the memories of deceased family members by having meals in their honor. New Christian families took up this custom by celebrating with special meals the anniversaries of the martyrs' deaths, as these were the days of their new births into heaven. In this way, Christians ensured that the memories of the martyrs' witnesses to the faith would not be forgotten.

At first, these commemorations of the martyrs' memories were done locally. The local churches created lists of those honored, and these became the first martyrologies. As the Church became more aware of its universal mission, Christians realized that the meaning a martyr had for a local church could be celebrated by the whole Church.

In 312, Constantine, a Roman general who was proclaimed emperor by his troops, won the battle of Milvian Bridge against one of his rivals. Constantine attributed his victory to the Christian God and, in 313, agreed with his fellow emperor from the eastern portion of the empire that there should be religious toleration of Christians. This was confirmed in the Edict of Milan.

With the public acceptance of Christianity, the commemoration of the martyrs became public. There were great celebrations, and memorial buildings were built and became shrines for prayer. There were banquets in early celebrations that were eventually replaced by prayer vigils, Scripture readings, songs, and preaching.

The relics of the martyrs, and later of the saints, were seen to have power over demons and to effect healing. Christians tried to be buried near martyrs so they could share in the power of the Resurrection. The relics of many martyrs were taken from their original burial sites to be housed in churches or basilicas. Prayer petitions were created for them, and the names of martyrs were given to Christian children.

Sainthood after the Persecutions

After the age of the martyrs, Christians looked for new ways to live and die in Christ. They found them in the monks and ascetics, men like St. Anthony, whose life became a model for

Christian life, and St. Pachomius, one of the founders of a monastic community.

The saints of this new age were men and women who cut themselves off from family and village and the temptations of sexuality. Called to a new Christian identity, the monks and ascetics went into the desert, where they prayed for the grace to overcome their personal temptations and live for Christ.

SAINT ANTHONY

Saint Anthony (251–356) was a major figure in early Egyptian monasticism. He had a comfortable childhood, spoke and read in Coptic, did not take to the surrounding Greco-Roman culture, and never learned the Greek language spoken in the areas where he lived.

When Anthony turned twenty, his parents died and he was put in charge of his young sister. Anthony placed his sister with a community of nuns and went into the desert, where he fought his personal temptations and practiced a life of self-sacrifice.

Anthony spent the rest of his life seeking solitude. He would settle at the edge of civilization, where followers would gather around him so he could give them spiritual direction for a time. He then would move further into the desert to re-establish solitude, and the cycle would start over. Later he would go to Alexandria to fight the Arian heresy. Finally he returned to a cave where he received visitors and gave spiritual advice until his death in 356.

Saint Athanasius (ca. 296–373), bishop of Alexandria, wrote a classic spiritual biography titled *The Life of Anthony*, a work that had profound influence in the spiritual life of the post-Constantinian Church.

SAINT SIMEON STYLITES

Another example of heroic faithfulness to God can be found in the life of St. Simeon Stylites the Elder (ca. 390–459). Simeon was born in northern Syria and entered the monastic life around 411.

Like Anthony, Simeon looked for a life of solitude and prayer. Syria, however, was a fertile and densely populated area; there was no desert for him to retreat to. People were aware of Simeon's dedication to God and personal holiness, and they came to him for counsel.

Since Simeon did not have enough room to create a place of solitude on the ground, he decided he would rise above the people. His fellow monks spent two years building him a nine-foot high limestone platform that was one yard square with just a handrail for safety. Eventually, the pillar would be sixty feet high. From this vantage point Simeon was separated from the people, so he was able to focus on prayer—but the people knew where to find him. Simeon served as counselor to kings and bishops and participated in the theological debates supporting the Church's teaching at the Council of Chalcedon (451). He continued to give counsel and advice until the day he died.

Saint Martin of Tours

Saint Martin of Tours was born about 316. Neither of his parents was Christian. His father was a tribune in the Roman army and, according to Roman law, Martin had to follow his father's footsteps into the army. He enrolled at the age of fourteen.

Martin first felt the stirring of faith at the age of ten. He became a catechumen and remained one while in the Roman army. Martin advanced quickly, becoming an officer at the age of eighteen. One day while on a winter march, Martin saw a man without a cloak. He immediately took off his own cloak, cut it in half, and gave half to the poor man. That evening in a vision, Martin saw Jesus wearing the half of the cloak he gave to the poor man. Jesus is reported to have said, "See! This is the mantle that Martin, the catechumen, gave me." Martin went immediately to be baptized.

When the bishop of Tours died, the people of the city brought Martin into town on a ruse, surrounded him, and demanded that he become their bishop. Martin was finally persuaded and became bishop of Tours in about 372.

As a bishop, Martin served as pastor in the city and preached the Gospel in the countryside, which at that time was largely pagan. He also traveled to plead for mercy for prisoners and to defend the faith against its detractors.

Martin was one example of a bishop whose life influenced the development of the Church in the Middle Ages. Martin's burial site became a place to which pilgrims came to view his grave and pray for healing.

SUMMARY

In the first centuries of the Church, the disciples of Jesus discovered that they were in a hostile environment in which their beliefs would be challenged. Christians were initially seen as an illegal sect and believers could be jailed and even put to death. The martyrs were the heroes of the early Church as witnesses who faced death to follow Jesus. As such, these men and women were remembered and venerated in the early Church.

As the Church became an accepted institution within the later Roman Empire, new forms of heroic sanctity emerged: the monastic retreat exemplified by Saints Anthony and Simeon Stylites, and the commitment to ministerial leadership demonstrated by Saint Martin of Tours. These examples show that there was no single road to a holy life, but that the commitment of Christian life calls men and women in every age to follow the call of God in their own time and place.

For Reflection

1. The martyrs valued their faith in Christ as more important than anything the world could give to them. When you think of the value of your Catholic faith in relation to the values of society today, name the things you would be ready to give up to be faithful to Christ.

2. Saint Anthony sought to discover himself and his relationship with God in solitude. How would you describe the value of solitude in helping you grow in your relationship with God?

3. Saint Simeon Stylites seemed to go to extremes in seeking to be alone with God. Yet he was considered a wisdom figure in his own time. Who are some people we can look to as today's wisdom figures for Church and society?

CHAPTER 4

Saints in the Early Middle Ages

The centuries from 500 to 1000 saw the Roman Empire in the West fall apart. Invading tribes from eastern Europe descended into Italy and Spain and across the straits of Gibraltar to northern Africa. An attempt by Emperor Justinian I (483–565) in Constantinople to retake the Western Empire had some initial success, but left behind devastated towns and villages.

The task of converting the tribes of Vandals, Lombards, Goths, Visigoths, and Franks was the work of centuries. To do this work, the Church had to move from the settled life of Roman civilization to life on the frontier. Converting the invaders included two tasks.

First, the Church had to overcome the Arian Christianity of the warrior tribes. The initial missionaries to the tribes were Arian bishops. When these bishops converted the tribes, they taught them that Christ was not equal to the Father. When these tribes invaded further into Roman territory, they persecuted the Catholic Church. Eventually, with the help of the Franks, the Church succeeded in overcoming the Arian influence. One way this was done was by emphasizing Christ's divinity in art and liturgy, creating the image of a distant and mysterious God. As a result, heroic saints like St. Martin of Tours were venerated because they helped to fill the gap between God and humankind.

Second, the Church entered into an alliance with Clovis (ca. 466–511), king of the Franks (the most powerful of the invading tribes), and converted him to the Catholic faith; however, it still had to convert the warrior tribes to Christian life. As Saint Gregory of Tours (538–594) described in *History of the Franks*, the Franks had created a vicious society. The nobility were violent and corrupt, ruling with brutality and contempt for any law; tribal values of loyalty and military honor were forgotten. Such a world was not open to intellectual argument. The Church could only impress the population by relying on its prestige as a spiritual power. Emphasizing the spiritual wrath of the distant God and judge was the only way to get the attention of the Frankish rulers.

Saints as Sources of Spiritual Power

In these times the saints were presented as sources of spiritual power to counter the fearsome power of the demonic and physical world. From their sanctuaries and shrines, the saints watched over the welfare of the land. The most important of these was the shrine of Martin of Tours. This was a place of healing where fugitives and political refugees could find sanctuary.

The example of the saints and the spiritual power they represented was the most important fact of life for the people. The saints, like Gregory of Tours and Pope St. Gregory the Great (540–604), were leaders of culture. They were influential in converting the common people, especially the peasants of the countryside who had not been influenced by the Christianity of the later Roman Empire. In many cases the cult to a local god was transferred to a cult to a local saint.

The literature of the saints in this period was filled with marvelous tales of healing and light. Gregory of Tours, for example, wrote *Miracles of St. Martin*, *Miracles of St. Julian of Brioude*, and *Glory of the Blessed Martyrs*. In contrast to the injustice that people faced in the everyday world, books like these revealed a world of mystery and divine power in which the terrors of everyday life did not dominate people's lives. In the world of the saints, nothing was impossible and no illness was too terrible that it might not be healed.

The stories of Christian saints, about the wonders of healing and protection, gave visible evidence to the power of the Church to overcome the world. Saints were a source of loving power and were actively involved in human life. They protected their own and defended the poor against injustice. The location of the saints' power was in the abbeys and pilgrimage churches.

SAINT GENEVIEVE

When Genevieve (422–500) was a young girl in the small village of Nanterre, near Paris, she attended a prayer service conducted by Germanus, bishop of Auxerre. Something in the child impressed Germanus, who predicted that Genevieve would live a saintly life. Genevieve then told Germanus of her desire to be blessed and consecrated to God.

At the age of fifteen, Genevieve was dedicated to God by the bishop of Paris. From then on she led a life of sacrifice and fasting, eating only on Sundays and Thursdays, and then only bread and beans. After her parents died, Genevieve went to live with her godmother in Paris. From there she became known as a prophetess and healer.

As the Franks moved to conquer Paris, the city suffered a long siege. Genevieve, moved by the suffering of the people close to starvation, led a company to bring food into the city and returned with boats loaded with wheat. Childeric, the king of the Franks, was impressed with Genevieve's bravery and sanctity, and allowed her to intercede on behalf of the lives of prisoners. Through Genevieve's influence, Childeric performed many other generous acts as well.

When Attila the Hun invaded Gaul in his rampage across Western Europe, ransacking Paris was one of his main objectives. Genevieve assured Childeric of God's protection and counseled the people of Paris to fast and pray. Without explanation, Attila changed course, went around Paris, and spared the city.

After her death, Genevieve was praised for the many miracles attributed to her intercession. The most famous of these was in 1129 when Paris was struck by a plague. When the bishop's call for prayer and fasting seemed to have no effect, the people carried the statue of Genevieve from her shrine to the cathedral. The plague disappeared. From that time to the French Revolution (1789), her statue was carried in all times of extraordinary distress. Genevieve's statue and relics were destroyed during the French Revolution.

Saint Boniface (ca. 680–754)

Although we do not know the exact date of St. Boniface's birth (ca. 680), we do know that he was martyred June 5, 754. Boniface belonged to a noble family in England and from his earliest days showed great intellectual ability. After receiving his family's reluctant permission, he entered the Monastery of Adescancastre, site of present-day Exeter. There, Boniface studied, was ordained, and joined the Benedictine community. Although he was being prepared for advancement, he was not ambitious for power. He wanted to become a missionary to convert the Saxons in present-day Germany.

Boniface went to Rome and eventually received the authority to spread the Catholic faith in Germany. Over the decades Boniface traveled through Germany many times, converting the pagans and bringing the baptized but poorly formed Christians back into the Catholic faith. He also founded monasteries and mission stations to help bring stability to the Church and to train the native clergy.

In the part of Germany called Lower Hessia, Boniface dramatically showed those who had lapsed into pagan beliefs the powerlessness of their gods. Boniface chopped down the oak sacred to the thunder god, Thor, and used the wood to build a Christian chapel dedicated to the Prince of the Apostles. The heathens were surprised and impressed by this show of spiritual power, since there was no thunderbolt from Thor to destroy Boniface. While Boniface continued to demolish pagan shrines, many were converted to the Catholic faith.

Boniface spent the rest of his life holding synods, training clergy and religious, mediating disputes between dioceses, praying, and meditating. In 754, he was on the mission train once again. After a successful year of conversions and baptisms in northern Germany, Boniface and fifty-two companions were attacked and murdered by pagan tribesmen. His body, recovered by his Christian followers who had escaped the ambush, was taken to Utrecht, then to Mainz, and finally to the great abbey at Fulda. His grave soon became a shrine to which the faithful came in crowds.

The Use of Relics

Relics are physical remains of the bodies of saints. The desire to be near the saints as persons of power led people to venerate the saints' relics as helps on the journey to salvation. In the days of the catacombs, the Eucharist was celebrated over the martyrs' bones on the saints' feast days.

The veneration of relics was quite popular in the early Middle Ages. This practice, however, sometimes led to superstition that assigned magical powers to the relics themselves. There was competition among villages over the relics of the saints, which included trafficking in relics and even the stealing of the remains of saints when one town thought the other was more prosperous.

Relics are still venerated in the Church as a legitimate form of Christian piety. The Church recognizes, however, that the veneration of relics and other personal devotions are meant to extend the liturgical life of the Church, not replace it. Thus relics should be venerated in such a way that clearly leaves the celebration of the liturgy superior to any personal devotion (see *CCC*, #1675).

The Prayer of Intercession

Prayers of intercession are prayers on behalf of other persons and their needs. The basis of the intercessory prayer is union with Jesus Christ, who is the one intercessor with the Father. United with Christ, Christians intercede for one another as an expression of the unity of people with one another under God.

Because Christianity is based on communion with God and others in Jesus Christ, Christians are called to care for one another in the deepest way, especially in praying for one another. This is all the more true for Mary and the saints. After Christ, Mary is the chief intercessor for all who are in need of Christ's grace. Mary and the saints offer prayers to God on our behalf.

Intercession is a fundamental form of prayer in the Church. It can be expressed in distinct petitions or can take the form of silently commending others to God. One important form of the prayer of petition is the offering of good actions to God on behalf of others. Our prayers and the prayers of the saints are joined with the prayer of Christ, the one who speaks for us in heaven (see *CCC*, #2634–2636).

❧✝❧

Summary

In the early Middle Ages (ca. 600–1100) in western Europe, peoples' lives were quite unsettled. Without a strong central authority, the people were at the mercy of whatever invading armies or raiding parties came through their villages. God seemed to be far away, and people lived in fear of the demonic world. In this terrifying world, the saints emerged as men and women who cared for the needs of the poor and who could intercede with God for the sake of the people. The shrines of the saints became places of pilgrimage; their relics became signs of the presence of the divine ready to do good.

This was a time in which intercessory prayer helped to form powerful bonds among Christians past and present. This time reminds us that we have a privilege and responsibility as believers to care for one another in commending the needs of others to God.

For Reflection

1. The Church had to work on the conversion of the invading tribes to Christian life. Some of the ways society must still be led to conversion today are . . .

2. The saints in the early Middle Ages were people who could make a difference in a hostile world. How can you influence society toward Christian values today?

3. One of the strongest values in Christian life is the power of intercessory prayer. Who are the saints you rely on to intercede for your needs in Christ?

CHAPTER 5

Mary in the Middle Ages

The spiritual climate in the Middle Ages created the need for the saints as personal intercessors for the people. That same climate is responsible for the emergence of Mary as the one to whom all could turn in times of trouble. We have seen how, in the Dark Ages, the Western European world was filled with constant war and threat of war. Powerful rulers fought one another for the right to oppress the poor of their territories. As the earlier tribes of Visigoths, Vandals, Franks, and others began to settle down, new forces continued to raid the settlements. From the north came the Vikings, who used the great river valleys of the Rhine and the Rhone to take their long ships into the interior to raid and pillage towns and churches and to capture slaves. From the east came the Magyars, horsemen from the Hungarian plains. From the Mediterranean came the followers of the new religion of Islam, who took North Africa and all of Spain, and raided into Europe until defeated by Charles Martel in 742.

The Importance of the Monasteries

In the midst of this turmoil between 700 and 1100, monasteries following the Rule of St. Benedict became islands of peace and sanctuary where civilization was preserved. In monastic scriptoriums, texts of all kinds—especially the Bible—were copied and thus preserved. All that we have of Latin literature in the West, for example, is found in the copies made in the monasteries during this period. In the 1100s, there developed in the monastic culture what scholars call the first renaissance of Western Europe, as the monks wrote about the values of individual contemplation and affective love expressed in friendship.

In this atmosphere, there began to emerge a new piety that would sing the praises and glory of Mary and reflect on her personal qualities. Saint Bernard of Clairvaux (1090–1153), for example, emphasized Mary's personal concern for the believer:

O man, whoever you are, understand that in this world you are tossed about on a stormy and tempestuous sea, rather than walking on solid ground; remember that if you would avoid being drowned, you must never turn your eyes from the brightness of this star, but keep them fixed on it, and call on Mary. In dangers, in straits, in doubts, remember Mary, invoke Mary.

(St. Bernard of Clairvaux , as quoted in
Virgin Wholly Marvelous, p. 121, #7)

Mary was celebrated in festivals on Marian feast days, to which the public was welcomed.

Growth of City Life

Cities began to grow once again in Europe in the 1100s. Universities were founded, beginning with schools of law and expanding into the liberal arts, to prepare students for the world of trade and commerce. Education, once almost totally given to monks and clergy, now found an audience among a growing bourgeois middle class. This meant that a spirituality now had to be developed for those who lived outside the monastic world. As a result, the mendicant orders, Franciscan and Dominican, were created. Members of these communities enjoyed more flexible living arrangements and trained in the universities in order to become the preachers for the emerging social classes.

The spirituality that developed in this age is more imaginative and human. The Christmas creche, for example, was created by St. Francis of Assisi in this period, and the suffering Christ on the cross became a central image in piety. Along with these images came the images of Mary as the loving and tender mother hovering over the manger, and the sorrowful mother at the foot of the cross.

Developing Images of Mary

The theology of the Middle Ages, influenced by St. Anselm's theology of atonement, emphasized the need for sinners not only to receive forgiveness for their sins but also to make restitution—pay damages, if you will—for the sins they had committed before the judgment of Christ. Even as he was being presented as the suffering Savior, Christ was being portrayed as the just judge waiting with the scales of justice to firmly place sinners where they belonged.

In these circumstances, Mary emerged as the tender and caring Mother of Mercy whose concern is to aid her children in joining her in heaven. This is the hope expressed in the great antiphon *Salve, Regina* (Hail Holy Queen), written in this period.

> Hail, holy Queen, Mother of mercy,
>
> hail, our life, our sweetness, and our hope.
>
> To you we cry, the children of Eve;
>
> to you we send up our sighs,
>
> mourning and weeping in this land of exile.
>
> Turn, then, most gracious advocate,
>
> your eyes of mercy toward us;
>
> lead us home at last
>
> and show us the blessed fruit of your womb, Jesus:
>
> O clement, O loving, O sweet Virgin Mary.

Believers then looked for the all-powerful protection of Mary, the Mother of Sorrows, who would understand their problems and would act as the helper in their time of need. Mary became a trustworthy confidant who would be the comforter and sure guide to heaven.

The Later Middle Ages

During the 1300s and 1400s, people felt a special need for a powerful friend. By 1360, the Black Death had killed a third of the population of Europe. In the later 1300s, there was schism in the western Church, with two—and later three—popes claming to have authority over the Church. In this world of death and confusion, Mary was honored as Queen of Heaven and Refuge of Sinners. She was the one who would bring just and merciful aid to all who came to her.

Mary's popularity in the Middle Ages was expressed in popular devotion. The people were delighted with the person of Mary and her position in God's plan for the world. A young girl from humble surroundings, she was chosen by God and declared to be "full of grace." God chose his mother not from the palaces of kings and queens, but from the quiet of a small village. It was she who shared the heart of God, she whose name they could sing about in songs of praise to God for what he had accomplished in her.

SAINT ANSELM OF CANTERBURY

Mary's decision to say yes to God meant that creation had a new chance. Picking up on the image of Mary as the new Eve, Mary's motherhood offered to all a second chance in life, for she was the mother of the Savior of the world. Saint Anselm (d. 1109) wrote that Mary's purity was so great, that none greater could be imagined:

> It was fitting that the conception of the Man Who was the Son of God should be by a Mother most pure. Fitting that the Virgin should be adorned with a purity than which none can be imagined greater below the Divine; the Virgin to whom God the Father decreed to give His only Son, Whom, begotten from His own Heart, equal with Himself, He loved as Himself, that entering the natural order He might become her Son as well as His; whom the Son Himself chose to make His Mother, substance of his

substance; of whom the Holy Spirit willed and decreed to effect that of her should be conceived and born Him from Whom He Himself proceeds.

(St. Anselm, as quoted in
Virgin Wholly Marvelous, p. 48)

The positive role of Mary in human life was expressed in poetry, hymns, prayers, and sermons. Anselm wrote that nothing was equal to Mary, and nothing but God was greater than Mary. As God is seen as the Father of all created things, Mary is the mother of all re-created things. Everything new and fresh in the world was related to Mary's re-creative presence. Mary was the sign of a new spring, of rejoicing spreading throughout the world, even to the gates of hell. Through Mary, light came into a dark world.

THE PRAISE OF MARY

Mary was celebrated in liturgical feasts, art, drama, and especially in the magnificent cathedrals built throughout Europe during this time. At Chartes Cathedral, for example, Mary is depicted as holding Christ as a small king in her lap. She is also depicted in the nativity scene, and over the north-central portal, Mary's death and awakening in Christ are sculpted. At the summit of the sculpture, Mary sits crowned in glory at the right hand of Christ.

The praise of Mary led people to Christ. In remembering her, people remembered her son who chose her and fashioned her to be his mother. Mary reflected the goodness of God, who loved the beautiful Virgin.

Mary as Mediatrix of Grace

Mary became known as the one who could help people on the road to salvation. She could mediate the mercy of God and be trusted to bring petitioners' needs before God. This developed into the theology of mediation and Mary's role as mediatrix of grace between believers and Christ. As such, she was pictured as being the aqueduct that brings the waters of the grace of Christ to believers.

Mary's role as mediatrix is related to the need for believers to hope in mercy. Christ was recognized as being the divine Savior but, as noted above, he was also seen as our judge. Believers feared they could not face the judgment of God without extra help from someone who could understand human weakness. For this, they leaned on the image of the Merciful Mother.

As our Merciful Mother, Mary embodied the virtues of sweetness, charm, and tenderness. No persons who had recourse to her would find that their faith had been placed in vain. Just as the Father listens to Christ, Christ listens to Mary. So sinners, by taking these little steps through Mary to Christ and on to the Father, would find the road to salvation a more hopeful path than they otherwise would have. In images of the Last Judgment in Christian art, Mary is seen kneeling before Christ to plead for sinners, a merciful sign before the throne of justice.

Believers felt that they always had a chance with Mary. She was the sure guide who could lead sinners and be merciful.

> In dangers, in troubles, in doubts think of Mary, call upon Mary. . . . If you follow her guidance, you will not go stray. If you pray to her, you will not give up hope. If you think of her, you will not do wrong. If she upholds you, you will not stumble. If she protects you, you will not be afraid. If she leads you, you will reach the goal.
>
> (St. Bernard of Clairvaux, as quoted in
> *Virgin Wholly Marvelous*, p. 118)

Reliance on Mary was expressed in many forms of popular devotion, such as *A Little Office of the Blessed Virgin Mary*, which celebrated Saturday feasts and Mass in her honor. The Hail Mary, said many times with genuflecting and prostrating, was prayed three times at the ringing of the evening bells. Associations were founded in Mary's honor and the singing of the *Salve, Regina* accompanied processions to monasteries and cathedrals.

Queen of Heaven

The need to have recourse to someone who would speak for believers in heaven led to the glorification of Mary as Queen of Heaven and Earth. Believers in the Middle Ages sought comfort and protection from Mary in the face of public and private disasters on earth. Disasters were not simply from natural forces or political conflict, however. The medieval world had a lively sense of the existence of a world of spirits, angels, and demons that were in constant conflict, and that influenced storms, droughts, wars, plagues, infestations of pests, and, ultimately, the eternal salvation of souls. The influence of the demonic was especially feared at the time of death, when the world of darkness had one last chance to capture the soul for hell. Under these circumstances, devotions, prayers to Mary and the saints, living a sacramental life, and giving to the poor were important practices in building up a fortress of protection against the battering forces of the demons.

The belief in Mary's Assumption into heaven was the foundation for the belief in Mary's queenship. Belief in the Assumption first appeared in the sixth century, when the feast day celebrating her death coincided with the appearance of the apocryphal stories collectively known as *Transitus Mariae*. This narrative purports to give details of the death of Mary, her funeral, the discovery of her empty tomb, and her bodily reception into heaven. As time went on, these images were developed in preaching and devotional literature. The medieval theologians reasoned that Mary's bodily Assumption was fitting because of her role as the mother of Christ; through his power as the Savior of the world, Christ could will the Assumption of Mary, he did will to do it, and he did it.

When Mary was received into heaven by Christ, she began to participate in his power over heaven and earth. In medieval times, heaven was modeled after a feudal court, with Mary in the role of Queen Mother. "The greatest glory of the blessed in Heaven is, after seeing God, the presence of this most beautiful Queen" (St. Peter Damian, as quoted in *Virgin Wholly Marvelous*, p. 106).

As people continued to approach Mary, her power to help was more and more drawn upon and praised:

> Her Son esteems her prayers so greatly, and is so desirous to satisfy her, that when she prays it seems as if she rather commanded than prayed, and was rather a queen than a handmaid.
>
> (St. Peter Damian, as quoted in
> *Virgin Wholly Marvelous*, p. 106)

All over Europe, believers appealed to Mary, while her relics and images filled cathedrals and country churches. Pilgrims flocked to her shrines, prayers were offered in her honor, and mystery plays made her the central attraction. In miracle stories, Mary's work for sinners would seem to move outside the law, making salvation possible for those who otherwise would not seem to have a chance.

> Why does the Church call Mary "the Queen of Mercy"? It is because we believe that she opens the abyss of the mercy of God to whomsoever she wills, when she wills, and as she wills; so that there is no sinner, however great, who is lost if Mary protects him.
>
> (St. Bernard of Clairvaux, as quoted in
> *Virgin Wholly Marvelous*, p. 107)

Mary's power seems to be so strong that even God would bend to her will. "At the command of Mary, all obey, even God" (St. Bernardine of Siena, as quoted in *Virgin Wholly Marvelous*, p. 108).

The Origins of the Rosary

The rosary developed in the Middle Ages as the Psalter of the unlettered. It was taught as a way for the people to participate in the praying of the 150 Psalms that were prayed in the Divine Office each week in monasteries. It began with people praying 150 Our Fathers, and expanded to include 150 Hail Marys, as that prayer became more popular.

The rosary as we know it today was developed in Carthusian monasteries in the 1300s and 1400s. It first developed with the scriptural verses of the Hail Mary. With time, little inserts reflecting on the life of Jesus were added after the name of Jesus. These inserts became the mysteries of the rosary, first with 50, then with 150 inserts divided into 3 sets of 50 each. Eventually, the mysteries were reduced to the present 15: 5 Joyful Mysteries, 5 Sorrowful Mysteries, and 5 Glorious Mysteries. The second half of the Hail Mary did not reach its final form until its use in the Roman Breviary in 1568.

In the later Middle Ages, the Dominican Order took the lead in spreading the devotion to Mary in praying the rosary. It was especially promoted by the Dominican Pope Pius V, who instituted the Feast of Our Lady of the Rosary in 1573, celebrating the intercession of the Blessed Virgin in delivering Christendom from the Turks in the Battle of Lepanto in 1572.

Summary

Devotion to Mary blossomed in the later Middle Ages. Mary was seen as the person who could intervene in mercy for believers who feared facing the just judgment of Christ. She was praised as Queen of Heaven, mediatrix of grace, Refuge of Sinners. Churches and cathedrals were built in her name and became sites of pilgrimages.

The enduring devotion to Mary that emerged from these times was the rosary. The rosary developed slowly during the Middle Ages during which time it was considered the breviary of the unlettered, a way in which all people could meditate on the mysteries of Christ and Mary. The rosary remains today a source of devotion and a way of praying that can be practiced by every believer in almost any time and place.

FOR REFLECTION

1. When would you find the *Salve, Regina* most helpful in your own spiritual life?

2. How does believing that Mary is the Queen of Heaven and Refuge of Sinners shape your sense of hope in salvation?

3. How do you hope that the Queen of Mercy might intercede for the needs of the world?

CHAPTER 6

Saints in the Later Middle Ages

During the Middle Ages, believers saw themselves entangled in a battle between spiritual forces, where on one side, God held indisputable power over the world as creator, savior, and judge, but on the other side, forces from the demonic world were attacking people. Individuals and communities alike needed all the help they could get from spiritual powers they felt understood them and their needs. The saints could provide this spiritual power.

Saints as Helpers

In the early Middle Ages, saints were acclaimed as important intercessors by popular proclamation. Interest in the saints was practical; saints were the ones who could provide the benefits people needed in life to survive this harsh world. They represented the spiritual power of the Church against all the forces of evil.

Proof of the effectiveness of the saints rested in their miracles. The memory of their virtuous lives was enhanced by miracles performed at their shrines and related to their relics. Saint Augustine, whose monumental work *The City of God* was one of the most important books influencing the Middle Ages, kept a record of saints' miracles as evidence of their place in heaven.

In the early Middle Ages, saints were most often proclaimed by the acclamation of the people, and their powerful influence was due to the popularity of their cults. As the Church became more institutionalized, and the papacy asserted more control over the local churches, the process of canonization of saints became more centralized. The publication of the *Decretals* by Pope Gregory IX in 1234 was a major move in this direction. The *Decretals* is a collection of papal laws in which Pope Gregory asserted the right of the Roman pontiff to have absolute authority in the naming of saints for veneration by the universal Church. Since saints were not just local figures, but were heroes for the universal Church, only the papacy—which has universal jurisdiction over the whole Church—could have authority to canonize.

Reforms of the Avignon Papacy

The Avignon Papacy (1309–1377) refers to that period of Church history in which the papacy, under the influence of the French monarchy, left Rome and settled in the city of Avignon in southern France. This was the height of the Middle Ages, and the papacy was becoming more and more institutionalized, with a growing papal bureaucracy and a more sophisticated legal system to rule the Church.

During the Avignon Papacy, the procedures of canonization became a legal trial in which candidates for canonization were represented by their petitioners and presented before the court by an official procurator or prosecutor of the cause. The papal side of the trial was led by a new position in the curia, the "Promoter of the Faith," more popularly known as the "Devil's Advocate." It was, and is, his task to investigate thoroughly any questions raised against candidates that might lead to a rejection of their candidacy for beatification or canonization.

Supporters of candidates for canonization had to gather evidence for their petition in the form of letters from kings, princes, bishops, and other prominent and honest persons. The will of the people, however, was no longer enough to satisfy papal demands. With these new procedures, trials might take months before any decision was made. Hundreds of witnesses might be called. As a result there were only twenty-six canonizations between 1200 and 1334.

Growing Popularity of Saints

In spite of the growing strictures in the canonization process, the popularity of the saints grew during the later Middle Ages; every village and town had its own patron saint. The rise of new religious orders and their close contact with the people added new candidates to the lists. In order to bring some clarity to the thriving interest in saints, the papacy began to make a distinction between those who could be venerated on the local level and those who would be venerated by the universal Church. Those who could be venerated locally or by their religious orders would be called "blessed." The title "saint" would be reserved to those persons recognized by the papacy as models for Christian life for the universal Church.

With these new rules and procedures, the reasons people were canonized began to shift. In the earlier years, canonization usually went to individuals who seemed to have proven themselves as public benefactors. Now those considered for canonization were more likely to be people dedicated to lives of fasting and penance, or who were intellectual defenders of the faith.

The goal of canonization became a matter of choosing those men or women whose lives seemed to be worth imitating. While evidence of miracles was not taken out of the process, it became more important to see candidates as examples of moral and spiritual virtue. By the middle of the 1200s, however, it became clear that simply leading a virtuous life was not enough. The standard became that of continuous, uninterrupted virtue, a life of perfection. While reformed sinners still had a chance for sainthood, people whose entire lives could be seen as lived in the grace of God proved to be better candidates for canonization.

As a result, when postulators for the cause of sainthood gathered evidence for a person's canonization cause, the pictures they drew of the candidate's sanctity became more idealized. The person was presented as almost without flaw, and the virtues of faith, hope, and charity were vividly described. Stories of the person came to include examples of supernatural gifts and showed how the candidate went to extremes in the practice of moral discipline.

As a result of these changes, sanctity in human life became identified with the intense and interior nature of the spiritual life. In the Middle Ages, this usually meant forgoing marriage and family life. The life of a person like Francis of Assisi became the model for Christian life.

SAINT FRANCIS OF ASSISI

Francis (1182–1226) was the son of Pica and Pietro di Bernardone. Pietro was a wealthy cloth merchant who wanted his son to follow him in the family business. Francis became a junior partner and enjoyed the life of wealth and prestige. Francis also had visions of military glory, but in a war with the neighboring city of Perugia, he was taken prisoner and kept captive for a year.

When Francis returned to Assisi, he suffered a long illness. Upon recovery, he discovered that he no longer had the taste for the high life that had been his habit before he went off to war. He increasingly led a life of penance, prayer, and almsgiving, which finally led him to sell some of his father's expensive cloth to fund his desire to rebuild a local chapel. His father was furious and brought Francis to judgment before the bishop of Assisi. In a dramatic gesture, Francis stripped himself of all the clothing he had received from his father and left in only beggar's clothing. He then spent several years caring for the poor and rebuilding local churches and chapels.

Francis had a vision in which he was told to build up God's Church, for it was falling into disrepair. Initially this vision moved him to work on the rebuilding of local chapels. Francis eventually realized, however, that he was being asked to rebuild the People of God. He began to preach, attract followers, and espouse a simple way of life based on the Gospels. In 1209, Francis and his followers formed a religious community, the Friars Minor, and received the tentative approval of Pope Innocent III. Francis sent his followers in small bands to preach, to work as day laborers, and to pray, leading others to conversion through word and example.

By the time of his death in 1226, Francis had over three thousand Friars Minor. He had traveled to Egypt to try to convert Islamic rulers to Christianity and had helped Clare found a Franciscan contemplative order for women. In 1224, after a profound mystical experience, Francis discovered that he had received the stigmata, the scars of Christ's passion, on his body.

Francis's genius as a catechist could be seen in 1223, when he built the first Christmas creche, in Greccia, Italy, as a catechetical example for the people to use to grow more closely in relationship with the human Christ. He sang to Brother Sun and Sister Moon, glorying in God's creation as a reflection of God's beauty. He is a saint who is loved by believers and nonbelievers alike—the patron of Italy, of merchants, of Catholic Action, and of the environment.

Saint Catherine of Sienna

In her short life, Catherine (1347–1380) had an immediate and historical impact on the world. The twenty-third of twenty-five children, Catherine began to have mystical experiences at the age of seven, and soon after pledged herself to Jesus. When Catherine rejected all attempts to find a suitor for her, her parents retaliated by releasing the family servants and assigning Catherine their household duties, thus giving her little time to pray.

One day, however, Catherine's father saw a dove hovering over her head while she prayed. Taking this as a sign of her vocation, her parents permitted Catherine to live a life of prayer and sacrifice. She practiced this in seclusion in her family home until she received a vision of the need to become active in the love she shared with Christ. Catherine entered into an apostolic life, caring for the sick, visiting prisoners, and accompanying those on death row to the gallows.

In 1375, while praying at the Church of St. Christina, Catherine had a vision of Christ and received the stigmata, wounds similar to those of Christ. From 1377 to 1378, Catherine composed her great mystical work, *The Dialogue*, offering her understanding of the Church and the sacraments. She praised the creative and saving love of God, of which the blood of Jesus was the greatest example.

Catherine was also influential in political life, negotiating a treaty between Florence and the papacy. She was outspoken in her support for the pope, and worked to convince the pope, who was residing in Avignon at the time, to return to Rome. Pope

Gregory XI, persuaded by Catherine's arguments, reinstated the curia in Rome but died before he could complete the move. Gregory's successor, Urban VI, was chosen in a disputed election in which the French cardinals said they were coerced. The French cardinals then elected a second pope, beginning the Great Schism that would last until 1417. Catherine supported Urban VI, although she was critical of some of his more irrational actions. Called by Urban VI to Rome to negotiate an end to the schism, Catherine died on the journey after great suffering.

Saint Catherine is a doctor of the Church, recognized by the Church as an eminent teacher of the faith. Her feast day is April 29.

Saints in the Later Middle Ages

Medieval Christianity was a culture of saints. Every trade, guild, village, town, and developing country had its own saints. People looked to the saints to ward off disease and evil spirits, and to guarantee good harvests. Pilgrimages and festivals multiplied, and lives of the saints became the most popular literature, images and relics of the saints attracting the illiterate.

By the early 1500s, however, some of the stories and practices had gone too far. For example, the catalog of relics of the archbishop of Mainz included a clod of dirt from the spot where Jesus recited the Lord's Prayer, one of the silver coins Judas was paid to betray Jesus, and the remains from the Israelites' manna in the desert.

Martin Luther (1453–1546) raised serious theological objections to the practices of the saints. He thought that the cult of the saints was idolatrous and pagan, and disputed the idea that saints had more grace than other Christians had. Luther insisted that since Christians are justified by grace alone, there was no treasury of merit from the saints that could be applied to Christian life. While he objected to exaggerations that had come into the literature of the lives of the saints, he had no problem with sober and accurate stories of the saints. Luther thought that next to the

Scriptures themselves there was no more useful book than the lives of the saints. However, he disputed that saints had any powers of mediation between God and Christians.

Council of Trent Responds to Luther

In response to the challenge of the Reformation, the bishops met in the Council of Trent (1545–1563) to deal with abuses within the Church. Among these abuses were bishops controlling more than one diocese, the sale of indulgences by Johann Tetzel in a carnival-like atmosphere, and the financial abuses in the papacy itself. The council met on and off for almost twenty years as political conditions allowed. Among its decisions was how to deal with the cult of the saints and relics.

At the Council of Trent, the Church reaffirmed the validity of veneration of saints and the proper use of relics. It accused those who rejected the mediation of the saints—especially Martin Luther and John Calvin—as having an irreligious mentality. In the reform that continued after the council, Pope Sixtus V created the Congregation of Rites in 1588 and gave it responsibility for preparing papal canonizations and the authentication of relics.

In the pontificate of Urban VIII (1623–1644) the papacy gained complete control over the process of canonization. In a series of decrees, Urban defined the canonical procedures to be followed for canonization. He especially decreed that there was to be no public veneration, publication of accounts of miracles, or revelations attributed to a so-called saint unless and until that person was beatified or canonized by the pope. This meant that all canonizations had to follow papal procedure. However, the decree did allow veneration of individuals who had been declared saints for at least one hundred years. The decree also stated that any unauthorized practice of a public cult to a person prior to beatification or canonization automatically disqualified that candidate for canonization. People could gather at the tomb to pray for that person's intercession, and they could pray in the privacy of their homes. Any public display of veneration, however, could lead to the cancellation of any future consideration for canonization.

The Process of Canonization Today

The evolution of sainthood has developed since the early Church, when saints were usually approved by acclamation—people simply proclaimed persons to be "saints" if those persons were seen to intercede for the people before God. Later, in the Middle Ages, this process was changed to include an examination that would determine whether the proposed saint had lived in ways that displayed cooperation with God's grace. Since the thirteenth century, this final judgment has been left to the pope alone.

Canonization is the term used for the process by which the pope officially sanctions and recognizes persons to be venerated as saints by the Roman Catholic Church. In recognizing persons as saints, the Church believes that these individuals have gone to heaven. Although they, like ourselves, were sinful persons in need of redemption, they practiced Christian virtue on a heroic scale, living lives that serve as beacons for fellow Christians on the road to salvation.

Present-day canonization follows rigid rules administered by the Congregation for the Causes of Saints. The process begins with the investigation by the local bishop of a person who has led a holy life or who has died a martyr's death. This usually follows reports that people have received help through this person's intercession in prayer.

Further investigation is then carried out by the Congregation for the Causes of Saints. If the person died as a martyr or is found to have lived a heroic life of grace, he or she is declared to be "venerable," and people may pray privately to the person and praise his or her virtues.

When a person has been venerable for a period of time, and it can be shown that a miracle has been performed after invocation in prayer, the pope declares the venerable person as "blessed." While this is not the last step in the canonization process, it does give moral certainty that the person who is "blessed" is in heaven. When a second miracle is authenticated in the name of the "blessed," canonization can follow.

The proclamation of the canonization of a saint is usually done with great ceremony at St. Peter's in Rome. The pope affirms that the person formerly named as "blessed" is a saint and worthy of veneration. The saint is a powerful source of intercession and an example for the universal Church.

Summary

Veneration of the saints grew during the later Middle Ages, so much so that this devotional practice would be severely criticized by Martin Luther as detracting from the true worship due to God alone. During this same period the Church codified the process by which saints would be proclaimed. The process of canonization today follows a long period of investigation to examine the claims put forward in the name of the candidate. If this candidate's case is successfully presented and accepted, there is a great ceremony in which another saint is proclaimed as an example to the faithful and a powerful intercessor for the needs of the people.

For Reflection

1. Who is the saint to whom you have most recourse?

2. Which saint do you think should be promoted for our time and place?

3. Research a patron saint for your occupation, country, or town. What are the qualities of this saint that you think are important to promote for the world today?

CHAPTER 7

Apparitions of Mary

As the Church entered the modern world, with its rationalist ways of thought, Christian people could have felt distanced from God. Society's principal image of God was that of a clock-maker who wound up the world and then left it to run on its own power without divine interference. In response to this challenge, the Church's theology was strongly academic and apologetic, matching any so-called proof against God with Aquinas's five proofs for the existence of God. While the theology of the times could be brilliantly done, it was also dry and difficult for most people to appreciate. On the local level, however, there was vivid preaching, like that of St. Alphonsus Liguori and St. Paul of the Cross, that could fill people's affective needs for God. People also found accessible ways to God in the reports of apparitions of Mary.

Apparitions are visions of Christ, Mary, angels, or saints reported by witnesses who see and hear the vision and transmit to others what they have seen or heard. There are a number of examples of apparitions in the Scriptures (see Tobit 3:16–17 and Genesis 26:24), the most important of which are the visits of the angel Gabriel to Zechariah, to announce the coming of John the Baptist, and to Mary, to announce the coming of Jesus (see Luke 1:11–22, 26–38). The apparitions that have been reported most often in the last centuries have been those of Mary.

Apparitions of Mary

There is no fixed location for the reported apparitions of Mary; they have been reported on all continents, by people of all ages from all walks of life. The places where Mary has appeared have come to be considered sacred, and can be found in cities, and in the countryside, in churches, monasteries, homes, caves, and other places.

The Church employs a long process in reviewing the validity of reported apparitions. The first important thing to realize is that messages and information revealed in apparitions are not new revelations. The authentic revelation of the Church is that which was entrusted to the apostles and transmitted to the Church (see *CCC*, #96). So a message given by Mary in an authentic apparition will not convey anything that is contrary to the teaching of the Church.

The Church classifies apparitions as "not worthy of belief," "not contrary to faith," or "worthy of belief." The process of classifying a reported apparition begins with the appointment of a committee by the local bishop. This committee investigates the incident by taking testimonies, studying the message that was given, and reporting to the bishop who initiated the study. The bishop then makes a ruling as to the supernatural character of the apparition. In making this judgment, the bishop must state that the apparition is not fraudulent, that the visionary is making true statements about the experience, that the experience cannot be explained away through natural causes, and that the experience is not demonic in origin. The magisterium seldom makes an official pronouncement about an apparition.

If the bishop makes a negative report about an apparition, the apparition is not to be believed. A positive report about an apparition, however, does not mean that the faithful are bound to believe that which is reported. If an apparition is approved, a devotional site can be created where people can pray and conduct devotions to Mary.

Eight Marian apparitions have been approved by the Church.

OUR LADY: THE VIRGIN OF GUADALUPE

The most important apparition reported in North America is that of Our Lady of Guadalupe. During the ten years following Cortez's conquest of the Aztec Empire of Montezuma in 1521, the Native Americans fell more and more under the heel of the Spanish conquerors. They were enslaved under the system of forced labor; millions died of smallpox. And the religion of the conquerors was forced on the people.

Juan Diego was an Amerindian peasant. One morning in 1531, while walking the Tepeyac, a hill outside Mexico City, he saw a beautiful lady who spoke to him in Nahuatl, the native language. The Lady told Juan Diego that she was the Virgin Mary, the Mother of God, and that she wanted him to take a message to the bishop. She wanted a church built on the hill in her honor. The Lady later appeared to Juan's dying uncle and healed him.

The bishop, Monsignor Zumarraga, met Juan Diego's report with skepticism; he also greeted Juan Diego's second message (of the Lady's encounter with his uncle) with skepticism. He asked for a sign.

When Juan Diego returned to the hill on December 12 to ask the Lady for a sign, he found flowers blooming on the ground even though it was midwinter. He gathered the flowers into his cactus-grass cloak and took them to the bishop. When he arrived and opened his cloak before the bishop, the flowers fell out. The amazed bishop and his staff then saw the picture of a young woman, surrounded by radiating light, imprinted on Juan Diego's cloak. This was the image of Our Lady of Guadalupe.

The image of Our Lady of Guadalupe combines images from two worlds. Her dress is European, but the decorations on the dress are Native American, and her face is mestizo. While the image has the aura of divinity, her facial expression is very human. In the image, Our Lady appears to be pregnant; over her womb is the symbol for the center of the universe, the symbol for Christ in the Nahuatl language. Mary is the God-bearer, pregnant with her divine Son.

The impact of Our Lady of Guadalupe on the life of the native peoples of Mexico was immediate and dramatic. In the image, they recognized a Christian presence that cared for them and their needs. Within the next two generations, eight million Aztecs would be converted to Christianity. In Our Lady of Guadalupe, the two cultures of the conqueror and the conquered were fused to form a new Christian experience for Native American Christianity.

Juan Diego's cloak bearing the image of Our Lady of Guadalupe, Patroness of the Americas, is now on exhibit in a large modern church, and is visited by thousands of pilgrims every year.

It has survived the blast of a bomb and the natural deteriorating effects of time, looking today as if it were freshly made.

SAINT CATHERINE LABOURE AND THE MIRACULOUS MEDAL

Saint Catherine Laboure was born in 1806 as Zoe Laboure, the daughter of peasant farmers. After the death of her mother when she was eight, Catherine helped her father raise her brothers and sisters. In 1830, her father allowed her to enter the Sisters of Charity of St. Vincent de Paul, where she took the name Catherine.

Soon after her entrance into the community, Catherine began to have visions of the Virgin Mary. In the most important of the visions, Mary appeared standing on a globe and surrounded by the words, "O Mary, conceived without sin, pray for us who have recourse to thee." The image also included a large letter "M," a cross, two hearts, and two crowns, all encircled by twelve stars. One heart represents the heart of Jesus, surrounded by thorns; the other represents the heart of Mary, with a sword driven through it.

The Virgin Mary told Catherine to have a medal cast with these images on the front and back. After the last of the visions in September 1831, and after receiving permission from the archbishop of Paris, Catherine had the medal struck in June 1832. The medal proved to be popular and became known as the "Miraculous Medal." Devotion to Mary of the Miraculous Medal was promoted by Fr. M. Aladel, Catherine Laboure's confessor.

For over forty years, Catherine quietly performed menial labor in the convent, speaking to no one about her visions until she was near death. Only then did she tell her mother superior of her visions. Catherine died December 31, 1876. Soon there were miracles attributed to Catherine Laboure's intercession, leading to her canonization by Pope Pius XII in 1947.

OUR LADY OF LA SALETTE

La Salette was a small village in France. In September 1846—two children Melanie Mathieu-Calvat, fifteen, and Maximin Giraud, eleven—were herding cows near the village when they saw a bright light and a beautiful Lady in brilliant clothing; the Lady was weeping. The children were told to give a message to the world. Mary called for a religious revival, for the people to repent—or the judgment of her Son against the sinful world would take place.

The children were also given a secret and were told to pray. Although there was only one apparition, a spring began to flow in that location and miraculous cures were reported. The local bishop conducted a five-year investigation and approved the cult to Our Lady of La Salette. However, the popularity of La Salette has never reached the heights of Lourdes or Fatima.

THE IMMACULATE CONCEPTION AND
OUR LADY OF LOURDES

The most popular shrine of our Lady in Europe is located at Lourdes, France; it receives some five million pilgrims annually. Lourdes is one of the great healing centers of the world, with reports of an average of one authenticated miracle every two years.

Lourdes had its beginnings in the apparitions of a Lady seen by Bernadette Soubirous, a girl from a poor family. Bernadette received eighteen messages between February 11 and March 25, 1858, in the garden of Massabielle. By the end of her experiences, some twenty thousand people had gathered to pray with her.

On February 24, the Lady told Bernadette to bathe in and drink from a spring near the grotto. Bernadette did as she was instructed, but the spring did not begin to flow where it could be seen by others until the next day. Since then it has been the source of miraculous healing. On March 24, the Lady told Bernadette that she wanted a chapel built in the honor of the Blessed Virgin. In her final apparition, the Lady told Bernadette her identity: "I am the Immaculate Conception."

Bernadette was subjected to four years of demanding examinations. Eventually, the apparitions were declared authentic on the basis of her testimony and the evidence of the miracles. For the rest of her life, however, Bernadette suffered the scrutiny of the curious. She entered the Sisters of Charity and Christian Instruction in 1865 and died in 1879. She was beatified in 1925 and canonized in 1933.

OUR LADY OF KNOCK

The apparitions in Knock, in the west of Ireland, were reported by fifteen people who witnessed a vision against the wall of the village church. The villagers reported seeing a lamb standing on an altar. In the background they saw figures that looked like angels. Three figures stood to the right of the altar. At the center was our Lady, with the figure of St. Joseph standing on the right and St. John the Evangelist standing on the left, holding a book. The vision was reported to have remained for a number of hours, but an official examination of the apparition reached no conclusion. In 1936, the report of a second commission was delivered to Rome, with no decision reached.

Through the work of two lay apostles, interest in Knock as a shrine was rekindled in 1936. A local Knock society was founded and the *Knock Shrine Annual* was published. Local bishops began to be supportive, and Knock received a variety of papal blessings, culminating in the visit of Pope John Paul II on September 30, 1979. On that occasion, the pope spoke to an immense crowd of pilgrims and made the newly built church of Knock a basilica.

Millions of pilgrims visit Knock every year to celebrate the Eucharist and to pray the rosary, the central spiritual activities of the shrine.

OUR LADY OF FATIMA

In Fatima, a small town in Portugal, three children—Lucia dos Santos and Francisco and Jacinta Martos (ages eight, seven, and six) reported seeing a veiled figure. This vision was followed by the appearance of an angel calling itself the Angel of Peace. The angel told the children to dedicate themselves to prayer, especially appealing to the hearts of Jesus and Mary.

The most important of the apparitions took place between May 13 and October 13, 1917. The children reported visions on the thirteenth of each month, except in August, when they were detained by a town official. Instead, they reported the vision on August 15.

The Lady in the visions, who eventually identified herself as the Lady of the Rosary, encouraged the children to pray the rosary daily. She told them to pray for peace and to dedicate themselves to the Immaculate Heart of Mary. The apparition of June 13, 1917, was especially important as the children were given a vision of hell and told that souls could be saved if devotion to the Immaculate Heart of Mary would be increased. Should this plea be ignored, an even greater war would break out, signaled by an unknown light appearing in the sky. Our Lady also asked the children to have people pray for the conversion of Russia. Without such prayer, Russia would spread its errors throughout the world, promoting war and persecuting the Church. These words about Russia were spoken to the children four months before the Russian Revolution.

On the final day of the apparitions, October 13, 1917, a crowd of about fifty thousand witnessed events that sealed the authenticity of our Lady's promises. The people saw the sun whirling in the heavens and leaving its orbit, plunging to earth. The impact of the event was to turn skeptics into believers.

Besides the exhortations to pray and the warning of future war, a third secret was given at Fatima. This secret message had been revealed to the popes since John XXIII, and was ordered disclosed by John Paul II in 2000.

Francisco and Jacinta Martos died in 1919, and Lucia entered a religious community. After a seven-year investigation, the bishop of Leiria proclaimed that the visitations were authentic and authorized the practice of veneration to Our Lady of Fatima.

Since then, three popes have honored Fatima. On the twenty-fifth anniversary of Fatima, Pope Pius XII consecrated the world to the Immaculate Heart of Mary. Pope Paul VI visited Fatima to celebrate its fiftieth anniversary in 1967. Pope John Paul II went on two pilgrimages to Fatima. The first occasion was on May 13, 1982, the anniversary of the assassination attempt on his life; the second visit was in 1991, to commemorate the tenth anniversary of his survival.

The message of Fatima is threefold: practice penance, pray the rosary, and practice devotion to the Immaculate Heart of Mary.

OUR LADY OF BEAURAING

The reported visions of Mary in Beauraing, Belgium, in 1932–1933 are less well known than the apparitions previously discussed. Mary is reported to have appeared thirty-three times to five children, ages nine through fifteen. These children were brothers and sisters: Andree and Gilberte Degeimgre and Albert, Fernande, and Golberte Viosin. The Lady identified herself as "the Immaculate Virgin," "Mother of God," and "Queen of Heaven." She told the children to pray for the conversion of sinners.

After an investigation, the bishop of Namur authorized the practice of veneration to Our Lady of Beauraing in 1943. The site of the apparitions is visited yearly by many pilgrims.

OUR LADY OF BANNEAUX

Another less well-known apparition is that of Our Lady of Banneaux. Eleven-year-old Mariette Beco reported a vision of Mary in the garden behind her family's cottage in Banneaux, Belgium. Our Lady is said to have appeared eight times and called herself the "Virgin of the Poor." Mary's message was a promise of intercession for the poor, sick, and suffering. The practice of veneration to Our Lady of Banneaux was approved by the local bishop in 1942.

THE CASE OF MEDJUGORJE

Medjugorje is located in Croatia, the Catholic region of the former state of Yugoslavia. On June 24, 1981, an apparition of the Blessed Virgin was reported by six young people: Vicka Ivankovic, Mirjana Dragicevic-Soldo, Marija Pavlovic-Lunetti, Ivanka Ivankovic-Elez, Ivan Dragicevic, and Jakov Colo-Jakov.

Since then, apparitions were reported at the original site where Mary is said to have appeared, as well as in the village church. In their visions, the children saw, heard, and touched Mary, and were given ten secret messages. As with other traditional apparitions, Mary called for greater faith, prayer, penance, fasting, and interior conversion.

Reports of the visions have led to some controversy. The local bishop, Pavo Zanic, did not believe the apparitions to be authentic, but rather a case of "collective hallucination." However, in 1986, Pope John Paul II approved pilgrimages to Medjugorje for the purposes of prayer, fasting, and conversion.

Medjugorje was the subject of a special meeting of the Yugoslavian Bishops Conference in April 1991. In their statement, the bishops said: "On the basis of the investigations so far, it cannot be affirmed that one is dealing with supernatural apparitions and revelations."

Noting the growing number of pilgrimages to Medjugorje that were taking place—a number rivaling that of pilgrimages to Fatima and Lourdes—the bishops further stated that they were willing to give assistance to the local bishop "so that in Medjugorje and in everything connected with it, a healthy devotion to the Blessed Virgin Mary may be promoted in accordance with the teaching of the Church."

A statement of the Congregation of the Faith, issued May 26, 1998, noted that the authentication of the events at Medjugorje would have to be reviewed by the newly organized Episcopal Conference of Bosnia-Herzegovina. Until that time,

> as regards pilgrimages to Medjugorje, which are
> conducted privately, this Congregation points out

that they are permitted on condition that they are
not regarded as an authentication of events still taking place and which still call for an examination by
the Church.

Norms for Authenticity of Apparitions

Apparitions and any messages given to the visionaries are officially "private revelations." As such, Catholics are not required to
give assent to the revelations or to the messages. In determining
the authenticity of "private revelations," the Church judges them
against revelation as expressed in Scripture and tradition as inter-
preted by the magisterium.

Norms for the discernment of the authenticity of apparitions
were issued on February 25, 1978, by the Congregation for the
Doctrine of the Faith. These "Norms of the Congregation for
Proceeding in Judging Alleged Apparitions and Revelations" were
approved by Pope Paul VI.

The "Norms" outline the responsibility of the local bishop to
conduct an investigation of the event with the aid of a committee of experts. The bishop's responsibility is based on his role as
chief catechist of the diocese as well as his responsibility for public worship. There are particular norms that the bishop can use to
discern the authenticity of visions.

First, the committee has to arrive at moral certainty, or at least
probability, that a miraculous event has occurred. This is arrived
at through interviews with the visionaries and relevant witnesses,
and a visit to the site of the event.

Second, the committee evaluates the personal qualities of the
visionaries. Are they mentally sound, honest, sincere, of good character, and obedient to ecclesiastical authorities? Do they participate in
the normal Catholic practices, such as reception of the sacraments?

Third, what is the message the visionaries are hearing in the
apparition? Is the message theologically acceptable; does it follow
the moral principles of the Church; and is it free from error?

Fourth, what are the long-term results of the experience? Are the changes in the visionaries and visitors to the sites enduring in terms of conversion, an increase in the ability to love others, and an ongoing fervent life of prayer?

The committee must have no doubt that what has occurred cannot be explained in any other way than being of supernatural origin. The teachings or messages given by the Blessed Virgin or the saint in apparitions must contain no doctrinal error. The visionaries must be seen as having no financial benefit from their visions. They must not be accused of immoral actions at the time of the visions, nor have any history of mental illness or psychopathic tendencies.

When he receives the report from the investigating committee, the bishop can make one of the following decisions:

1. The event shows signs of being authentic, a miraculous intervention from heaven.

2. The event is clearly not miraculous, or the evidence is insufficient to judge it so.

3. There is no evidence that the event is miraculous.

The bishop does not have to make a clear judgment on the miraculous nature of the event to allow public worship to take place at the site of the event. Such public worship can be carried out if it is done in good order as the investigation continues.

Regarding the responsibility of the faithful, members of a diocese are to obey their bishops, who serve as Christ's representatives (see *Code of Canon Law*, #212). This obedience is owed to the bishops as they are the leaders of the local Church and are responsible for promoting the common good. The faithful are also called to give "religious assent" to their bishop's teaching authority, and owe intelligent obedience to the bishop in terms of his decisions regarding the authenticity of apparitions.

Summary

The number of apparitions of Mary in the past few centuries shows her continued care for the world and the need of her people to invoke her intercession. It is important to understand the principles used to certify an apparition as a valid devotion to Mary and to obey the bishops whose responsibility it is to carry out this task.

For Reflection

1. Which appearance of Mary do you find most meaningful?

2. How do you understand the principles of judging the validity of apparitions? What are the ways in which you can discern what is an authentic apparition?

3. What do you think is your responsibility in following the teaching of the bishops about giving personal assent to a reported apparition?

Mary and the Saints in the Modern World

On July 25, 1959, Pope John XXIII announced his intention to call a council to review the state of the Church. The council was convoked on December 25, 1961. Four separate sessions met between October 1962 and December 1965. During the council, the whole life of the Church was reviewed and the role of Mary in the life of the Church was reassessed.

Mary and the Second Vatican Council

Preparations for the Second Vatican Council included the development of schemata, or drafts, on the place of Mary in Catholic belief. The bishops and consultants were thinking that there would be a separate document on Mary. The central commission accepted the 1700-word schema entitled *Mary, Mother of God and Mother of Men*. The fathers of the council decided not to present this during the first session.

At the beginning of the second session of the council, in September 1963, the opening debate dealt with whether there should be a separate schema on Mary or whether she should be included in *Lumen Gentium (LG)*, the *Dogmatic Constitution on the Church*. The speaker for inclusion, Cardinal Koenig of Vienna, argued that a separate document of Mary could give the impression that the council was presenting new dogma on Mary. It was important that Mary be treated as a member of the People of God. Inclusion in *LG* would assure that Mary would be seen in her role as a type or model of the Church, her saving role resembling the saving role of the Church.

Placing Mary within *LG* would also have the advantage of avoiding the impression that the cult of Mary was somehow not related to the Church. Eastern Catholics would recognize the importance that the Church was placing on Mary as *Theotokos*, and Protestants would be sympathetic in the scriptural and ecclesiological grounding of the place of Mary within the Church.

The arguments of Cardinal Koenig prevailed by seventeen votes, the narrowest majority in all the votes on the council. It took another year of work, however, to get the schema ready for inclusion into *LG*.

Chapter 8 of *LG* connects Mary to Christ, noting that she belongs to the "race of Adam" and "is at the same time also united to all those who are to be saved" (#53). At the same time, Mary "is hailed as pre-eminent and a wholly unique member of the Church, and as its type and outstanding model in faith and charity" (#53). The document then relates Mary to the Old Testament, where Mary

> is already prophetically foreshadowed in the promise of victory over the serpent which was given to our first parents after their fall into sin (cf. Genesis 3:15). Likewise she is the virgin who shall conceive and bear a son, whose name shall be called Emmanuel (cf. Isaiah 7:14; Micah 5:2–3; Matthew 1:22–23). She stands out among the poor and humble of the Lord, who confidently hope for and receive salvation from him. After a long period of waiting the times are fulfilled in her, the exalted Daughter of Sion and the new plan of salvation is established, when the Son of God has taken human nature from her, that he might in the mysteries of his flesh free man from sin. (#55)

Picking up on the patristic theme of Mary as the new Eve, the document continues, quoting the early fathers:

> "The knot of Eve's disobedience was untied by Mary's obedience: what the virgin Eve bound through her disbelief, Mary loosened by her faith." Comparing Mary with Eve, [the Fathers] frequently claim: "death through Eve, life through Mary." (#56)

Mary's own life was a "pilgrimage of faith." The document reviews Mary's journey with Christ, from the announcement of his birth to her place at the foot of the cross, where she is proclaimed by Christ to be the Mother of the Church, mother of all believers (see *LG*, #56-58).

Section three of *LG* chapter 8 discusses the relationship of Mary to the Church. Here the document tackles the relationship of Mary to Christ who is the one mediator between God and humankind. The document makes clear that the graces that flow from Mary do not originate from Mary herself, "but in the disposition of God." What Mary shares with us is the "superabundance of the merits of Christ, [that] rests on his mediation, depends entirely on it and draws all its power from it." Mary "does not hinder in any way [our] immediate union . . . with Christ but on the contrary fosters it" (#60).

Mary's role in the salvation of humankind did not end with the cross. It continues to intercede for us to bring the graces of salvation. Mary cares for all those "who still journey on earth surrounded by dangers and difficulties, until they are led into their blessed home" (#62). Because of her constant intercession, Mary is invoked under the titles of Advocate, Helper, Benefactress, and Mediatrix: "This, however, is to be so understood that it neither takes away from nor adds anything to the dignity and efficaciousness of Christ the one Mediator" (#62).

Section four of *LG* lays down the principles under which the cult of the Blessed Virgin may be practiced. It notes that the cult increased in popularity following the definition of Mary as the Mother of God at the Council of Ephesus. It also supports all the devotions to Mary in which

> while [she] is honored, the Son through whom all things have their being (cf. Colossians 1: 15–16) and in whom it has pleased the Father that all fullness should dwell (cf. Colossians 1:19), is rightly known, loved and glorified and his commandments are observed. (#66)

The Second Vatican Council recommends that the devotion to Mary be "generously fostered," and that devotion and other pious exercises that have developed in the history and tradition of the Church be "religiously observed."

The council also cautions the faithful:

> Carefully refrain from whatever might by word or deed lead the separated brethren or any others whatsoever into error about the true doctrine of the Church. Let the faithful remember moreover that true devotion consists neither in sterile or transitory affection, nor in a certain vain credulity, but proceeds from true faith, by which we are led to recognize the excellence of the Mother of God, and we are moved to a filial love towards our mother and to the imitation of her virtues. (#67)

Mary's power of intercession does not extend to the faithful alone. Her life is one of intercession for the world, until all families of people, whether they are honored with the title of Christian or whether they still do not know the Savior, may be happily gathered together in peace and harmony into one People of God, for the glory of the Most Holy and Undivided Trinity. (#69)

Marialis Cultus

In 1974, Pope Paul VI wrote the apostolic exhortation *Marialis Cultus (MC), For the Right Ordering and Development of Devotion to the Blessed Virgin Mary*, a document developing guidelines for the renewal of popular devotion to Mary. Paul VI established the following guidelines for valid devotions to Mary. First, the devotion should be rooted in the Bible and imbued with the great themes of the Christian message.

> This will ensure that, as they venerate the Seat of Wisdom, the faithful in their turn will be enlightened by the divine word, and be inspired to live their lives in accordance with the precepts of Incarnate Wisdom. (*MC*, #30)

Pope Paul VI also notes that the situation of women today calls for theologians to rethink the meaning of Mary for the modern world.

> The picture of the Blessed Virgin presented in a certain type of devotional literature cannot easily be reconciled with today's life-style, especially the way women live today. In the home, woman's equality and co-responsibility with man in the running of the family are being justly recognized by laws and the evolution of customs. In . . . politics, women have in many countries gained a position in public life equal to that of men. In the social field, women are at work in a whole range of different employments, getting further away every day from the restricted surroundings of the home. (#34)

Paul VI realized that the image of Mary as the passive, humble maid does not sit well with many women in the modern world. "In this regard . . . theologians, those responsible for the local Christian communities, and the faithful themselves [are exhorted] to examine these difficulties with due care" (#34).

The pope had suggestions in this regard. First, he suggested that Mary be presented as an example of the faith, not in terms of her sociocultural background, but "for the way . . . she fully and responsibly accepted the will of God (cf. Luke 1:38), because she heard the word of God and acted on it, and because charity and a spirit of service were the driving force of her actions" (#35).

Second, when examining the devotions to Mary that have grown up over the centuries, the Church "does not bind herself to any particular expression of an individual cultural epoch or to the particular anthropological ideas underlying such expressions" (#36).

Third, Paul VI notes the positive ways in which Mary could be appreciated in the modern world, based on what we find in Scripture. For example, the Mary we find in the Gospels is a woman who is willing to make decisions that will have an impact on the direction of the world. "[She] gives her active and responsible consent, not to the solution of a contingent problem, but to [an] 'event of world importance,' . . . the Incarnation of the Word" (#37). Mary's choice for living a consecrated life of virginity was for the sake of dedicating her life totally to God.

Finally, Mary speaks for the needs of the poor:

> She was a woman who did not hesitate to proclaim that God vindicates the humble and the oppressed, and removes the powerful people of this world from their privileged positions (cf. Luke 1:51–53). The modern woman will recognize in Mary . . . a woman of strength, who experienced poverty and suffering, flight and exile (cf. Matthew 2:13–23). These are situations that cannot escape the attention of those who wish to support, with the Gospel spirit, the liberating energies of man and of society. (#38)

Mary and the Latin American Episcopate

This theme of the liberating power of Mary's prophetic role is found in the final document in the Third General Conference on the Latin American Episcopate meeting in Puebla, Mexico, in 1979. In the document titled *Evangelization in Latin America's Present and Future*, the bishops write:

> The *Magnificat* mirrors the soul of Mary. In [it] we find the culmination of the spirituality of Yahweh's poor and lowly, and of the prophetic strain in the Old Testament. . . . In the *Magnificat* she [is] the model for all . . . those who do not passively accept the adverse circumstances of personal and social life and who are not victims of "alienation" . . . but who instead join with her in proclaiming that God is the "avenger of the lowly" and will, if need be, "depose the mighty from their thrones." (#297)

Pope John Paul II and Mary

The role of Mary is a consistent theme in the writings of Pope John Paul II. In all of his major writings, Mary is found as an example to follow, as an intercessor to be invoked, as a person whose blessings we seek. Mary is given special attention in John Paul II's encyclical, *Redemptoris Mater (RM)*, "On the Blessed Virgin Mary in the Life of the Pilgrim Church."

As we enter the new millennium, Pope John Paul II notes that while progress in science and technology seems to move human life faster and faster into the future, humankind still is subject to the transformation of "falling" and "rising":

> It is also a constant challenge to people's consciences, a challenge to man's whole historical awareness: the challenge to follow the path of "not falling" in ways that are ever old and ever new, and of "rising again" if a fall has occurred. (*RM*, #52)

On this journey, humankind is assisted by Mary, an ever-present sign of God's care for all people of goodwill.

> [The Church] sees Mary deeply rooted in humanity's history, in man's eternal vocation according to the providential plan which God has made for him from eternity. She sees Mary maternally present and sharing in the many complicated problems which today beset the lives of individuals, families and nations; she sees her helping the Christian people in the constant struggle between good and evil, to ensure that it "does not fall," or if it has fallen, that it "rises again." (*RM*, #52)

Saint Thérèse of Lisieux

Thérèse of Lisieux was born in 1873, the youngest of nine children of whom five daughters survived. Her parents, devout French

Catholics, raised their family in an atmosphere of devotion and service to others. Because her mother died when Thérèse was quite young, Thérèse was raised by her father and older sisters. When her oldest sister, Pauline, left home to become a Carmelite sister, Thérèse was devastated and became ill. Through her family's prayers and the intercession to Mary, she was cured.

All of Thérèse's sisters eventually entered religious life. Two older sisters became Carmelites, and one became a Poor Clare. Thérèse was anxious to follow in their footsteps and wished to enter Carmel at the age of fourteen. In spite of resistance, she was admitted at the age of fifteen and spent the last nine years of her life as a religious. Her sister Celine stayed home to take care of her father and entered the convent after he died.

When Thérèse became a nun, she dreamed of doing heroic deeds. She dreamed of going to Indochina and dying as a missionary, and she dreamed of becoming a priest. But neither of these was the life to which she was called. Rather, her life was to be one of daily dedication to God in the circumstances in which she lived.

Thérèse learned to detach herself from anything that got in the way of her relationship with God. She let go of her lifestyle as a pampered child with its pets, lessons, and summers on the shore. Her desire became to live a "hidden" life.

Living in close proximity with her community, Thérèse learned that detachment meant doing small acts of love, such as smiling at someone she did not like or eating the food set before her without complaining. This was not just substituting "little acts" for "heroic acts." It was a moving away from all sense of accomplishment—even in the smallest of things. She strove for an inner attitude of remaining little, certain that God was upholding her from moment to moment.

By the time she died, Thérèse had also learned the meaning of detachment regarding her death: she gave up any expectation that she might die the death of a saint. For the last years of her life, she suffered from tuberculosis of the bone but refused to make her illness a reason to be unkind to others. Thérèse did not expect any special ecstasy or experience in her dying. She identified only with Jesus, the victim who died in agony and redeemed others in his act of love.

Thérèse detached herself from her early dreams of glorious martyrdom but did not become bitter over her circumstances. She kept her core ideal of offering her life to God, even to the moment of her death. Instead of dying the heroic death of a martyr, however, she died from tuberculosis, the most common death in Europe. She even joked about it as she prepared for death. A month before she died, she noted how ironic it was that while she desired martyrdom, it was apparent that she would die in bed.

THÉRÈSE'S LIFE OF PRAYER

In Thérèse's spiritual environment, prayer was something someone said according to fixed formulas. One said or recited prayers from ancient times and tried to imagine Jesus as he lived centuries before. Thérèse believed that Jesus and the Father were listening at the moment she was praying. Everything she said mattered because she was in a living relationship. And as in life, the relationship was of change. Thérèse's prayers were spontaneous conversation. She would talk to God when she was happy, sad, or sleepy.

In the last years of her life, Thérèse prayed without experiencing any sense of joy or happiness. At the very time when she ceased to pray for specific favors from God, symptoms of her tuberculosis began to appear. Thérèse believed without question that God would grant anything she asked, but thought that it would simply be her own childish desire to ask. She did not pray for a cure or even that she might be spared the pain she was experiencing. Thérèse's prayer was dry, and she stated that Jesus wasn't doing anything to keep the conversation going. In her grief, she would fall asleep in prayer, consoled by the thought that just as children were loved as they slept in their mother's arms, God must love her as she slept in prayer.

THÉRÈSE'S EXPERIENCE OF DARKNESS

In the midst of her suffering and the dryness in her prayer life, Thérèse did not lose her sense of trust in God. She trusted with the sense of trust that we find in the psalms: a trust that did not hope for things to get better in the future. In the midst of temptation not to believe, she trusted.

Thérèse's relationship with God was not static, rather it was an ongoing encounter of God from moment to moment. While she might have had intellectual doubts about particular beliefs, her abiding trust in God kept her from ever despairing.

LOVE AT THE CORE OF THÉRÈSE'S LIFE

Thérèse realized that a person could be the most proficient technical practitioner of all the elements of spirituality, but without love, that person's life would be empty. She also realized that God called her to love right where she was, in her little community of hurt and rigid people (see O'Connor, *In Search of Thérèse*, pp. 161–162). Her writing reflects these realizations:

> *I understood it was Love alone* that made the Church's members act, that if *Love* ever became extinct, apostles would not preach the Gospel and martyrs would not shed their blood. I understood that LOVE COMPRISED ALL VOCATIONS, THAT LOVE WAS EVERYTHING, THAT IT EMBRACED ALL TIMES AND PLACES . . . IN A WORD, THAT IT WAS ETERNAL! . . . Then, in the excess of my delirious joy, I cried out: O Jesus, my Love . . . My *vocation*, at last I have found it see. . . . MY VOCATION IS LOVE!
>
> (St. Thérèse of Lisieux, as quoted in *Story of a Soul*)

It was love that kept Thérèse close to Christ in the last months of her life, during the terrible temptations against faith and the temptations to suicide. In the hours before her death, she summed up her life in terms of love:

Never would I have believed it was possible to suffer so much! never! never! I cannot explain this
except by the ardent desire I have had to save souls.

(Clarke, *St. Thérèse of Lisieux:
Her Last Conversations*, p. 205)

THÉRÈSE'S DEATH AND CANONIZATION

Thérèse's sister Pauline, prioress of the community, told Thérèse
to write down her experiences. After Thérèse died, Pauline sent
two thousand copies of a heavily edited version of her book,
Story of a Soul, to other Carmelite communities. Thérèse was
praised as the "little flower," and the impression was that her spirituality was sentimental and timid. With complete editions of
her works now widely available, we see that Thérèse's spirituality
was lived and written about within a life of suffering. Anything
but sentimental, she was firm in her convictions and dedicated to
truth in her relationships with others and with God.

Beatified in 1923, canonized in 1925, named principal
patroness of missions in 1927, Thérèse, with Joan of Arc, was
also declared secondary patroness of France by Pope Pius XII in
1944. In October 1997, Pope John Paul II also declared Thérèse
a doctor of the Church.

WHAT THÉRÈSE OFFERS THE MODERN WORLD

Thérèse is a saint for everyday life. In her short life she recognized
that the place where she could love God and fulfill her vocation
was where she was each day. Reflecting on her life, we can see that
the heroic need not be defined in terms of great deeds and spec-
tacular accomplishments. Thérèse's "little way" of reaching out to
her Carmelite family is a model for each person in every family,
workplace, parish, and neighborhood. Thérèse helps us see that we
are called to God in the midst of life, not in trying to escape it.

Summary

In their documents on Mary since the Second Vatican Council, Popes Paul VI and John Paul II emphasize the continuing importance of Mary for Christian life. St. Thérèse provides a more recent example of what it means to be a saint. Mary and the saints continue to be companions on our Christian journey.

For Reflection

1. How do you see Mary walking with us in this new millennium?

2. The emphasis of the Latin American bishops on Mary's commitment to the oppressed and needy reminds us that our attitude toward the poor should be . . .

3. When you are faced with your own frustrations in daily life, how can the example of Thérèse help you recognize what God is calling you to today?

Conclusion

The story of the development of our understanding of Mary and the saints, and their roles as intercessors in our lives, is a fascinating blend of history and spirituality. This history reveals the Catholic belief that those who lead holy lives, past as well as present, are committed to helping others on the journey to salvation.

In his exhortation to America, Pope John Paul II especially commends to Catholics the memory of Mary and the saints as helpers on the journey. Of Mary, he wrote:

> How can we fail to emphasize the role which belongs to the Virgin Mary in relation to the pilgrim Church in America journeying towards its encounter with the Lord? Indeed, the Most Blessed Virgin "is linked in a special way to the birth of the Church in the history . . . of the peoples of America; through Mary they came to encounter the Lord." (*EA*, #11)

As patroness of the Americas, Mary will continue to hold the attention and devotion of the people of the United States.

Beginning with the canonization of Saint Rose of Lima (1586–1617) in 1670 by Pope Clement X, the list of those who have been declared saints and blessed continues to grow.

> The beatifications and canonizations which have raised many sons and daughters of the continent to public veneration provide heroic models of the Christian life across the range of nations and social backgrounds. In beatifying or canonizing them, the

Church points to them as powerful intercessors made one with Christ, the eternal High Priest, the mediator between God and man. (*EA*, #15)

In his apostolic letter *Tertio Millennio Adveniente (TMA)*, "On the Coming of the Third Millennium," the pope notes that the blood of martyrs continues to be shed for Christ. Their memories should not be forgotten:

The local Churches should do everything possible to ensure that the memory of those who have suffered martyrdom should be safeguarded, gathering the necessary documentation. (*TMA*, #37)

So, the need for Mary and the memory of those who live wholeheartedly for God are not to be forgotten, but remembered by us all as fellow travelers and helpers who journey with the faithful on the road to God.

Abbreviations

CCC   *Catechism of the Catholic Church*

EA   *Ecclesia in America (On the Encounter with the Living Jesus Christ: The Way to Conversion, Communion, and Solidarity)*

EN   *Evangelii Nuntiandi (On Evangelization in the Modern World)*

GDC   *General Directory for Catechesis*

LG   *Lumen Gentium (Dogmatic Constitution on the Church)*

MC   *Marialis Cultus (For the Right Ordering and Development of Devotion to the Blessed Virgin Mary)*

RM   *Redemptoris Mater (On the Blessed Virgin Mary in the Life of the Pilgrim Church)*

TMA   *Tertio Millennio Adveniente (On the Coming of the Third Millennium)*

Bibliography

Buby, Rev. Bertrand, SM. *Mary, the Faithful Disciple.* Mahwah, NJ: Paulist Press, 1985.
   A study of the New Testament portrait of Mary. Mary is presented as a model for Christian discipleship and faithfulness.

Catechism of the Catholic Church. Washington, DC: United States Catholic Conference, 1994.
   Summary of the Catholic faith, a "sure and authentic reference text for teaching Catholic doctrine."

Clarke, John, trans. *St. Thérèse of Lisieux: Her Last Conversations.* Washington, DC: Institute of Carmelite Studies, 1977.
   Supplementing Thérèse's *Story of a Soul,* this book contains Thérèse's final interviews with her sisters in the last critical months of her life.

Congregation for the Doctrine of the Faith (Archbishop Tarcisio Bertone, Secretary to the "Congregation"). Letter to His Excellency Monsignor Gilbert Aubry, Bishop of Saint-Denis de la Reunion, May 26, 1998.

———. (Joseph Cardinal Ratzinger, Prefect of the "Congregation"). "The Message of Fatima," June 26, 2000.

Coyle, Kathleen. *Mary in the Christian Tradition.* Mystic, CT: Twenty-Third Publications, 1996.
   Mary is presented as a strong, active, resilient woman of faith and a model for Catholics seeking to express their faith today.

Cunneen, Sally. *In Search of Mary: The Woman and the Symbol.* New York: Ballantine Books, 1996.
   Traces the development of devotion to Mary through the last 2,000 years.

de La Portierie, Rev. Ignace, SJ. *Mary and the Mystery of the Covenant.* New York: Alba House, 1992.
    A study of Mary in the Scriptures and her place in the mystery of the covenant with God and his people.

Donnelly, Doris, ed. *Mary: Woman of Nazareth.* Mahwah, NJ: Paulist Press, 1989.
    A series of essays by theologians who explore the history and development of Marian theology.

General Directory for Catechesis. Washington, DC: United States Catholic Conference, 1998.
    Provides the fundamental theological and pastoral principles for the coordination of the catechesis in today's world.

Grassi, Joseph, A. *Mary, Mother and Disciple: From the Scripture to the Council of Ephesus.* Wilmington, DE: Michael Glazier, 1988.
    Traces the development of Marian theology from New Testament times to the Council of Ephesus in 451.

Lukefahr, Oscar. *Christ's Mother and Ours.* Liguori, MO: Ligouri, 1998.
    An overview of the importance of devotion to Mary for the life of the Church.

O' Carroll, Michael. *Theotokos: A Theological Encyclopedia of the Blessed Virgin Mary.* Wilmington, DE: Michael Glazier, 1988.
    A comprehensive theological encyclopedia of Catholic thinking on Mary.

O'Connor, Patricia. *In Search of Thérèse. Vol. 3 of The Way of the Christian Mystics.* Wilmington, DE: Michael Glazier, 1987.
    A classic study of St. Thérèse that shows her special contribution to spirituality in the twentieth century.

Pope John Paul II. *Ecclesia in America (On the Encounter with the Living Jesus Christ: The Way to Conversion, Communion, and Solidarity).* Washington, DC: United States Catholic Conference, 1999.
    Pope John Paul II's post-synodal apostolic exhortation presenting the blueprint for future efforts in ministry for the Church in America.

————. *Redemptoris Mater (On the Blessed Virgin Mary in the Life of the Pilgrim Church)*. Washington, DC: United States Catholic Conference, 1987.

Pope John Paul II's encyclical on Mary and her importance for the Church.

————. *Tertio Millennio Adveniente (On the Coming of the Third Millennium)*. Washington, DC: United States Catholic Conference, 1995.

Apostolic letter of Pope John Paul II to help Catholics prepare for the Jubilee of the year 2000.

Pope Paul VI. *Evangelii Nuntiandi* (On Evangelization in the Modern World), 1975.

————. *Marialis Cultus (For the Right Ordering and Development of Devotion to the Blessed Virgin Mary)*. Washington, DC: United States Catholic Conference, 1974.

Pope Paul VI's encyclical that expresses the importance of Mary being presented in ways that can speak to the condition of women in the modern world.

Second Vatican Council. *Lumen Gentium (Dogmatic Constitution on the Church)*, 1964.

Supple, David, OSB, ed. *Virgin Wholly Marvelous: Praises of Our Lady by the Popes, Councils, Saints, and Doctors of the Church*. Cambridge: The Ravengate Press, 1991.

An anthology of statements about Mary from popes, councils, and saints through the centuries.

Third General Conference on the Latin American Episcopate. *Evangelization in Latin America's Present and Future*, 1979.

Woodward, Kenneth. *Making Saints: How the Catholic Church Determines Who Becomes a Saint, Who Doesn't, and Why*. New York: Simon and Schuster, 1990.

A study of how saints are made, examining social, political, and religious influences in the process of canonization.

Acknowledgments

The Scripture quotations contained herein are from the New Revised Standard Version Bible, Catholic edition copyright © 1993 and 1989 by the Division of Christian Education of the National Council of the Churches of Christ in the U.S.A. Used by permission. All rights reserved.

English translation of the *Catechism of the Catholic Church* for the United States of America copyright © 1994, United States Catholic Conference, Inc.—Libreria Editrice Vaticana. English translation of the *Catechism of the Catholic Church: Modifications from the Editio Typica* copyright © 1997, United States Catholic Conference, Inc.—Libreria Editrice Vaticana. Used with permission.

Excerpts from *Virgin Wholly Marvelous: Praises of Our Lady by the Popes, Councils, Saints, and Doctors of the Church* edited by David Supple, O.S.B. ©1991, Ravengate Press, Still River, MA are used by permission of the publisher. All rights reserved.

Excerpt from *Evangelization in Latin America's Present and Future* ©1979 by Consejo Episcopal Latinoamericano (CELAM). Used with permission.

Excerpt from *In Search of Mary: The Woman and the Symbol* by Sally Cunneen ©1996 used by permission of Ballantine Books, a Division of Random House, Inc. All rights reserved.

Excerpt reprinted with permission from *Mary in the Christian Tradition: From a Contemporary Perspective*, by Kathleen Coyle. Copyright © 1996. Published by Twenty-Third Publications, Mystic, CT 06355. Toll free: 1-800-321-0411.

Excerpts from *Vatican Council II, Volume 1, Revised Edition: The Conciliar & Post Conciliar Documents* edited by Austin Flannery, O.P. copyright ©1998, Costello Publishing Company, Inc., Northport, N.Y. are used by permission of the publisher, all rights reserved. No part of these excerpts may be reproduced, stored in a retrieval system, or transmitted in any form or by any means – electronic, mechanical, photo-copying, recording or otherwise, without express permission of Costello Publishing Comany.

Excerpt from *In Search of Thérèse*, Vol. 3 of The Way of the Christian Mystics by Patricia O'Connor ©1987, is reprinted by permission of the author.

Excerpts from the English translation of *A Book of Prayers* © 1982, International Committee on English in the Liturgy, Inc. All rights reserved.

About the Author

James P. Campbell, D. Min., is Staff Theologian for Loyola Press of Chicago. For eight years, James served as director of the Orange Catechetical Institute, responsible for adult education and formation in the Diocese of Orange, California. He was also consultant for catechetical curriculum development for the Office for Religious Education, Archdiocese of Chicago. He is general editor of Harper's New American Bible Study Program. His other writings include *The Third Millennium: A Catholic Perspective*, published by NCEA, and *Understanding Scripture: The Genesis Creation Story*, published by Loyola Press.